A Suzie Story

By

Suzie Cole

ISBN: 978-0985374969
ISBN-0985374969

A Suzie Story
Copyright © 2015
Suzie Cole

Cover design by Thomas Shamburger
Cover photography from Suzie's Family Albums

Proven Justice Inc.
POB 232
Winona, TX 75792

E-mail:Honory@aol.com

For additional family pictures go to Suzie Cole Facebook.

Published by: Proven Justice Inc.

Printed in USA

ISBN 978- 0985374969

Dedication

To my family
And
All those who have made my life worth living.

Acknowledgements

Thanks to all who contributed their time and energy and made this book possible.

Contents:

A Suzie Story & The Accident
Introduction

If every day of your life were a page in a book, in sixty-five years you would have 23,725 pages. For most of us page 5,652 would look much like page 22,387. So, rip out the duplicate pages and, while we are at it, let us remove the mundane and skip through the average days. This leaves us with a book of the highs and lows of our life. In the case of *A Suzie Story*, it leaves us with a complex character with a most interesting life.

I hit the wall of writers block. I was spending too much time staring at a blank computer screen. Sister Suzie, mentions she put her life stories to pen and desires to create a book. "It needs to be brought to life." You hold the results.

Remember, two people can see the same thing and walk away with two different stories. Time also reshapes memories more to our liking. The dialogue is created from Suzie's writings and my own imagination. The real name of the giant Saudi Arabian turtle remains a mystery.

The Accident will help you to appreciate those who have suffered and survived.

A Suzie Story is a treat for those who know her and those who will never see or meet her. It is a timeless story that spans the globe and three husbands. Richer, poorer, happiness and tragedy: get ready for Suzie's rollercoaster life.

Within these pages, I learned much about myself and you will too.

So, is Suzie a saint, sinner, or both? You decide.

Thomas Mitchell Shamburger

The Accident

Prologue
By: Suzie Cole

Posted on Facebook:

February 2008:
On the way home from Winona, Texas, to Scottsdale, Arizona, a car accident occurred in a small town called Colorado City, Texas, on the Loraine Bridge – at approximately 8:45-9:00 am. Here is what we know: there was ice on the bridge, a red Dodge Ram truck lost control and began to spin. Suzie (62 YO) and Ron Cole (77 YO) came upon the vehicle and hit it head on at 60 mph. A third vehicle, a large diesel truck, lost control and slid across the icy bridge – stopping just short of hitting Suzie and Ron. A fourth vehicle hit the diesel truck. In a split second everything changed.

"How has your life been?"
Before the accident, I would have flippantly answered, "Great!"
A Suzie story consisted of here and now. History was what happened yesterday and the future is what will happen tomorrow. Much like a teenager!

Looking back on my life, I considered it average: three marriages, three divorces, with few great moments. No stardom or great accomplishments were on my résumé.
I am a child of God! I have known this since early childhood. I have sought God and studied His Word. I

have drawn strength and peace from God. With a Christ centered life, I felt my life was one of great fulfillment.

Christ in you, the hope of glory. Colossians 1:25-27, *New International Version* (NIV)

If God is for us, who can be against us? Romans 8:31, (NIV)

Did I use these scriptures as a shield to protect me, or, did I use them as a shield to hide behind, all these years?

Then, *The Accident* happened. During two years of recovery, my life, family, faith, and future all came into question. After recovery, I found myself still dealing with new thoughts and emotions.

I tried to write about what happened. I would stop when I started writing my own name. With a pen in hand or, looking at a computer screen, I could not see myself, Suzie, in such a broken and suffering condition. I had never truly looked back to the life-changing events of those two days, two months, two years... I struggled; tears flowed even though it had been years since *The Accident*. Still, I had a burning desire to tell my story.

Elizabeth came to the rescue. I do not know why I chose the name, Elizabeth. I had an Aunt named Elizabeth but we called her Aunt Diddie. By letting Elizabeth take my place, I was able to continue writing my story. I was able to be on the outside looking in.

By writing, I found I was dealing with emotions trapped inside. I also realized how much I enjoyed just sitting down and reliving the past. I may have embellished or added to some of the stories. Perhaps my memory is tainted with what I want to believe.

Possibly grandchildren and future generations might appreciate knowing who this crazy lady, Suzie, really was.

I soon found out the appeal of the story reached far beyond my own kin.

Therefore, I must give thanks for *The Accident*. This particular story caused me to develop a great love for writing. This is a typical response for the eternal optimist that I am.

Some will read this book for inspiration, but most will read it for entertainment. I hope you are inspired and entertained. I also pray you learn a little something as I share my life with you.

"How has your life been?" you ask.
"Read the book!" is now my answer.

I still act like a teenager every now and then.

God Bless,
Suzie

The Accident
Part 1
Elizabeth View

"Mother, we don't want breakfast. We have had a delightful two weeks and you had a wonderful birthday!" says Elizabeth. "Now, we are leaving early in the morning without any fanfare or goodbyes."

Time and time again, family and friends ask Elizabeth, "Please wake us up before you leave." No, Elizabeth always chooses to leave mysteriously before dawn.

Her mother, Evie Leola McClenny Shamburger, was the reason Elizabeth made the trip from Scottsdale, Arizona.

Leola became Lolo upon the arrival of her first grandson. "Lo-lo-Lo-lo-Lo-lo," Arden called her and Leola became, "Lolo."

Lolo's birthday party was combined with the Winona Methodist Churches Prayer Room dedication. In front of a large congregation, each of her grandchildren spoke candidly of times past, giving glimpses of their memories with LoLo.

Granddaughter, Lena, made an honest and stunning comment with her recollections and put it this way:

"Lolo is the personification of practicality with a touch of elegance."

"LoLo could be comfortable dining with the president of the United States and she could be just as comfortable serving or eating with the poor and homeless." That might be a requirement of a true saint!

Elizabeth is ready to go. As soon as Lolo's big birthday celebration was over, she began mentally packing the Caravan.

So much good "stuff", Elizabeth thinks, and she keeps adding more. She loads a nice antique table with an old matching chair. There is a large beautiful stained glass window given to her by a dear friend, Glenn. He spent many hours creating it. They carefully pack the treasured art piece in layers and layers of plastic bubble wrap.

"I think the middle of the Caravan is the safest place," said Glenn.

Last and least, but not least in value, is a gorgeous large Waterford Crystal vase. It is wrapped in multiple clothing for protection. Elizabeth has entrusted this vase in her mother's care for years. To Leola's dismay, she has decided it is time to take it home and enjoy it herself.

Of course, there is luggage, books, knickknacks, tools, a set of wooden bowls and silverware, a wardrobe of clothes that moves from place to place, a designated space for the ice chest and on top of a cardboard box full of more stuff is the doggie bed.

By Friday night, the van is loaded to the brim!

In the darkness, Elizabeth quietly takes the ice chest to the refrigerator and starts loading it up with Dr. Pepper and snacks. Then comes the ice and ice is loud. Everyone knows you cannot quietly fill an ice chest! The quieter you try to be, the louder ice gets. Closing the lid, she listens, hoping to hear nothing.

"That means you too." She hears her husband, Ron, talking to Cleo and Buffy, their Pekingese dogs.

Elizabeth sits down at the little kitchen table to write a note of gratitude and love. It is the last thing she always does when leaving her mother's small apartment.

Elizabeth hears the clatter of dog claws on the door as Ron opens the front door. Two little dogs scamper out the door as soon as they will fit through the opening and Ron follows.

> Mother,
> Another wonderful visit. Thanks for the hospitality. This trip was great. I got the Waterford vase because you are getting old and the grandkids are putting their names on everything. The vase is mine! I figure if I left early enough, you couldn't stop me. Ha.
> Love you much and will call tomorrow. Good Lord willing.
> As always,
> Elizabeth

Elizabeth leaves the note, as usual, on the dining table. Leola will easily see it when she wakes up in a few hours.

Cleo and Buffy are sitting up in the doggie bed. They look at Elizabeth as she climbs in the Dodge Caravan.

"Fifteen-hundred miles and we're back in Scottsdale," says Ron as he starts the motor.

"Wait, I forgot my jewelry! I have to sneak back in." Elizabeth loves her jewelry. She remembers the time she and sister, Perry, went into a jewelry store. The girl tending the counter said in a long southern drawl, "I can tell you girls sho does like yo gold!" Elizabeth does wear a lot of jewelry, more than most people do, but that is just the way she is.

Three minutes later in the cool early morning, Ron

sees the small silhouette run back to the car with a cross necklace and all the other jewels she would never leave behind.

"Mission accomplished, this time for sure," she says. "Let's pray. Lord, come with us now as we head home. Keep us safe from harm and we pray a sweet spirit will accompany us all the way. Thank you Lord. Amen."

As soon as they roll onto Interstate 20, Cleo jumps into Ron's lap. Cleo and Buffy love to ride in the driver's lap. Elizabeth settles back and waits for the sunrise so she can read.

Six hours later, they are two-thirds of the way across Texas. Buffy is now the lap dog. It is much colder in this part of Texas and there are ice patches on some of the bridges. Elizabeth notices Ron clench the steering wheel and looks forward. They are on an icy bridge.

"Keep your foot off the brake, just try to get into the other lane," Elizabeth shouts. That is what she has been taught all her life. Then, all sounds stop and in slow motion the van feels like it is floating across the bridge. Elizabeth sees a huge red truck drifting, head on toward her. The sound of metal crunching and glass breaking shatters the outside silence.

The air bag explodes in her face and there is considerable pressure from the dash. Elizabeth goes limp and closes her eyes. All is dead still and she feels at peace, much like the quiet after a storm.

"Is that a child screaming in the distance?" It is not a hurting cry, but one of shock or surprise. Elizabeth says this only in her mind and she realizes that she is not moving and barely breathing.

"Cleo, is that you?" Elizabeth looks up and Cleo

licks her in the face. She pushes her back and Cleo bounces around with her little tail wagging so hard her rear-end shakes back and forth. "Why are you so happy?"

"I'm going to Heaven!" says Cleo. Elizabeth is shocked. In eight years, she has never heard Cleo, or any other dog, say a word!

"When did you learn how to talk?" Cleo jumps through the broken windshield and is gone.

"Wake up Elizabeth!" She hears Ron and he seems far away.

"You have to move," she says to herself. "It's time to take charge of things. What to do first? Breathe! Why is it so hard to breathe?"

Her eyes open and she silently talks to herself. "What else is there to do but look around and assess what is happening?" Like waking up from a bad dream, she looks around and raises her left arm. Her hand dangles earthward: the wrist is swollen bigger than a softball. She looks at it and with a loud cry shouts, "My wrist, it broke my wrist!"

She decides it is time to move but she cannot. She is stuck, pinned down by her seatbelt and dashboard. It is tight, too tight! Taking her right arm and drawing her hand close to her waist, then scooting it through the cramped area in front of her, she is able to push the seatbelt latch and cause it to release! "Yes, that's better; now I can breathe."

In what seems like a very few minutes, help arrives. The passenger door is forced open with the Jaws of Life, by the Colorado City Volunteer Fire Department. Mitchell County Emergency Medical Services swiftly take Elizabeth out of the van. They lay her on a backboard face up. A very fine rain mist is coming down and it is a welcome coolness on her face.

Questions, questions, and more questions from the medical team.

"What is your name?"

"Suzie. I mean Elizabeth!"

"Do you know your address?"

"Scottsdale, Texas, I mean Arizona."

"Tell us your phone number!"

"Nine-O-three, I mean four-six-eight, three, seven, seven, nine, two, four, three, two, one...."

"That's too many numbers."

"Seven, seven, sev--en, se--v---en..." She begins to mumble.

The medics remain persistent, "You've got to talk to us! We need for you to stay alert as much as possible. If you want to live, speak up... What are you saying?"

With an extra effort she says, "I'm talking to God. I'm talking to God." A feeling of solitude rushes over her and she peacefully repeats, "I'm talking to God."

"Talking to God is good. But now you must talk to us if you want to live."

Elizabeth starts speaking calmly and slowly. "It will be ok if I don't live. Everything will be fine if I go to be with God." She closes her eyes and prays, "Praise God for those professional people who are trained and know what to do at times just as this one."

As she drifts into a peaceful sleep, she hears the ambulance driver yell, "Come on, and bring your dog with you. We have to go."

They say that when you die your whole life flashes before your eyes. Maybe that is why some people stay alive longer than others.

A Suzie Story
By Suzie Cole

Chapter 1
Childhood

World War II is ending. US Army Staff Sergeant Thomas Jefferson (T.J.) Shamburger is overseas in the Philippians. His wife, Leola, is living with her parents close to the Brazos River, near Cameron, Texas. Many wives went to their parents while their husbands went off to war.

Evie Leola McClenny became Mrs. Shamburger eight years earlier. Slim, but not petite, wavy hair and a beautiful smile made Leola someone all the guys went after. Also, Leola was a foot washing Baptist raised with a sister and a wild brother.

T.J. was a rambunctious young man with a mischievous smile and a twinkle in his eye. He was one who would not take no for an answer. That twinkle caught Leola and as two opposites attract, the two came together. Her slim build made her beautiful but difficult to have children. She gained 8 pounds during this pregnancy. A little over six pounds belonged to me. I was inside, comfortable and did not want to come out.

For the last three days, Leola has not been at home with her five and a half year old daughter, Perry Jo. She is in the hospital. There have been three days of cramping, contracting, pushing, relaxing, and breathing: child labor.

I arrive as Gerry Sue Shamburger, and given the nickname, Suzie. When I hear "Gerry Sue," I most assuredly know I am in trouble! Either a doctor is returning my call, the IRS is checking up on me, or a family member is very mad! Otherwise, Suzie it is.

Daddy receives the telegram three months later! "To: Sergeant Thomas J. Shamburger: You have a daughter. Gerry Sue Shamburger. Born: November 19, 1945."

"Suzie cried the first two years of her life," says Mother. "She was hanging to my apron, clinging to my dress or snuggling next to me all the time. If I stepped away from her…get ready for screams and tears."

With his military commitment behind him, my father returns home and we move back to East Texas. Winona is a very small East Texas town near Tyler, the "Rose Capitol of the World." Winona was the early stomping grounds of Mother and Daddy. They grew up and went to high school in and around Winona.

Daddy works in the family business of growing, processing, and shipping roses. We live in a large, run down, two-story house, which we inherited from Granddaddy Perry Shamburger. It sits right in the middle of Winona. The old home place is the perfect spot to be. We know and see almost everything that goes on in town!

I am blessed to have Christian parents and many friends. In a city with a population of less than five hundred, everyone knows everyone! Not only do you know your neighbors, you know your neighbors business as well! This is not a bad thing. The citizens are more like family and they share each other's burdens and joys! We have a "party-line" telephone. This means other telephone conversations go over the same wires as yours. You may, inadvertently, listen in on your neighbor's phone conversation, or you might join in. After all, it is called, "a party-line."

T.J. and Leola are very close to several couples with children my age. Family life is a simple formula for everyone: grow up, get married, and have two or three children. This is my world.

Victor and Lorene Kay are my parent's best friends. Their daughter, Vicki, is my sister's age and their son, Brent is almost a year older than I. Their brick home is in viewing distance from our house. It is the only brick house in town. Kay's Grocery is the largest store in Winona. Our families are in touch every day.

Wendell and Margie Dale, another of my parent's good friends, live just past the Kay house. They later built a brick house right across the street from ours. Kathy, their daughter, is my age. Kathy and I have exciting times together. We spend our summers exploring the streets of town, riding our bicycles, playing cards and enjoying board games. These games can last for as long as three days. The simple life of a child is great!

The Kays, the Dales and other Winona families join in many activities.

The Sabine River runs through East Texas and often, weekends would find us "down on the river." According to a brief history of Hawkins published by the Chamber of Commerce, "Belzora was a river port as well as a stagecoach crossing from the 1850's until the coming of the railroad. Many came to Wood County over this crossing. Felix Wells operated a ferry."

The Sabine River changed course, maybe thousands of years ago, and created Lake Belzora. When my Granddaddy Perry was a young man, he and his brothers, bought Lake Belzora and divided it among themselves. A dam created a second larger lake and we call it all, "The Shamburger Lakes." It continues to be passed down, undivided, to each generation.

I remember friends and families going to the lakes; the men fish, drink beer, and cook, while the women play bridge. We had fun fishing, swimming and just exploring the junglish surroundings. We spent many nights in one of the old lake houses that stood on stilts overlooking the lake. Memories galore as I think back on those days of my early childhood. Mosquitoes, primitive toilets, snakes, and even swimming with alligators did not seem like a big deal during my childhood.

I knew of two churches in the town of Winona, The First Baptist Church and The First Methodist Church, separated only by Church Street. There were no air conditioners and heat was not an excuse to miss church. So, with triple digit heat, the windows were raised in the summer time. This let the air in and the sound out. The piano and organ combined with the voices of the congregations, from both churches, brought smiles to everyone's face. It would sometimes cause confusion. We used to joke that the Methodist would be singing, "Will there be any stars in my crown?" while the Baptist would echo their song of, "No not one! No not one!"

Every Sunday the trumpets would sound, the ground would shake, and not from the Holy Spirit. It was the eleven-fifteen clanging of the Cotton Belt Railroad train going through downtown and drowning out the singing in both churches. Each Sunday, the train passed through Winona. I wonder if the engineer was unaware of the disturbance or did he smile and blow the trumpets an extra time or two? *The train schedule has not changed and is heard every Sunday in the four churches of Winona!*

The Methodist and Baptist churches are a block from our house. Sunday mornings we walk past The First Baptist Church of Winona on the way to The First Methodist Church of Winona. The local streets are bustling with people making their way to receive their weekly spiritual boost. Sunday school is at ten and the main Church service at eleven. All across America, all church services are at this time! To me, this is the times set for all the church services of the world. It was my tradition!

Mother sends my sister and me to Sunday school early and she arrives in time for the main church service, with or without Daddy. Daddy makes it to church at least once a month. He insists that WE go every Sunday.

I adore Sundays and I love learning about God the Father, Son and Holy Spirit. At an early age, I know I can depend on my faith throughout the rest of my life. I marvel at the teachings of Jesus. I want to be a missionary when I grow up!

PRAISE
Sing praise to the Father
Sound praises to the Son
Give thanks for the Holy Spirit
Praise God for the three in one!

How gracious and good is this God of ours
We lift our hearts in prayer.
Almighty God, yes, God of love
He knows our every care!

With light and beauty my spirit sings
New life my body beholds.
Enjoyment, fulfillment and blessed peace,
As each new day unfolds!

The Lord refreshes with new supply,
When dilemma blinds our sight.
The Father's compassion refills our cup
And replaces the "burnt out" light!

Suzie

I am crazy about people. Anytime I see one or more kids playing outside, I immediately head in that direction. My time is spent bicycling, playing hopscotch, jump roping, or just climbing the best tree in town. This tree happens to be on the corner of Dallas and Kay Street, where we live! We call it The Snake Tree.

The Snake Tree is a gorgeous huge wisteria vine which, in full bloom, is a massive burst of purple petals that look like grape pods delicately hanging. Most assuredly, its beauty takes the breath of everyone who drives up Dallas Street. Often, unbeknownst to passersby, we children are comfortably sitting in the tree on the branches, hidden beneath those blooms! I spend many hours cradled in that tree which serves as playhouse, clubhouse, hideout, or simply my place to sneak when I desire to be alone.

In 1950, kindergarten is not an option for a five year old. In fact, we have never even heard of kindergarten. Six-year-old children started the first grade. *There was no Day Care, as there was no need for Day Care. Men were the breadwinners and women raised the children, did domestic chores and maintained the household.*

"But why can't I go to school? Brent is going. I am as smart as Brent!" I cry.

"Honey," Mother tries to comfort me, "Brent is six years old. When you are six you can go to school."

"Brent goes to school and I am left behind?"

Like Daddy, I will not take "NO" for an answer. I insist on starting school, even though I am only five. My parents make it happen!

I am a tiny five-year-old. I weigh twenty-five pounds and am in the first grade. I look ridiculous trying to keep up with all of the others while running and playing. I may be small on the outside but not on the inside.

The playground is not my main problem. My fear and insecurity returned. The first six months of school, I cry and insist on sitting on my teacher's lap during every recess!

Mrs. Lilly Brown taught Mother as a child. She lived at Mother's home for room and board. Mrs. Brown is like family and she is my first grade teacher. She treats me as though I am her own.

Looking back, I think having God's favor may have had something to do with the outcome of my blessed first grade experience.

Everyone in the city limits walks to and from school. Each afternoon we leave school looking for our mothers. Twice a week the social ladies of Winona gather for a long game of bridge at one of their homes.

In 1952, Daddy and Mother surprise us with a baby brother. Thomas Mitchell Shamburger was born on September 20. I am almost seven years old and no longer the baby of the family.

"Why do I have to give in to the baby?" *I still ask that question!* With my easygoing personality, I accept this and adjust easily.

I love to spend time with my friends. Alice Faye Jackson is one of them. During the summers, I join her on short family trips. In turn, she goes with me to my grandparents. During the school year, we take turns spending nights at one another's house.

A particular memory is my observance of the interaction between Alice Faye and her father, John. He would come home in the evening after a long day of working at the family owned sawmill. Alice Faye would crawl into John's lap. She would cuddle there as they enjoyed discussing events of the day. I watched that scene with envy. My father certainly did not have a knack for showing affection. I have no memory of Daddy ever sitting down and having a fun or a loving conversation with me as a child.

Many friends have come and gone. The friends I have mentioned have remained steadfast as lifelong "best friends." We seldom communicate personally, but through our family members and mutual acquaintances, we keep apprised of each other's wellbeing.

.

The summer months without school are definitely the time I favor each year. We play outside until after dark. It is one of the privileges of living in a small southern town. Parents do not fear, nor even consider, that danger lurks among the children as we play in the streets.

It was a different age, an atmosphere of innocence.

Today, in the same town, parents keep a much closer watch over their children. That freedom from fear was prevalent; those days have disappeared. What a sad truth we see as time and change continue to march on!

At times, we catch lighting bugs early in the evening. We squeeze the light out of them and stick that gooey glowing light on our fingers making beautiful rings. We do not think twice about squeezing the guts out of those bugs!

Can those poor lighting bugs be the beginning of my obsession with the shine and brilliance of jewelry?

Every summer we look forward to a week in Galveston! Galveston is a long six-hour drive from Winona. Families often meet us there and rent a cabin beside ours. The cabin doors stay unlocked. In the 1950's, there is no need for locked doors.

"Where do you think you're going?" Mother ask Brent and me.

"We are going treasure hunting." It is not the first time Brent and I have explored the Gulf of Mexico.

"Don't you two wander off too far," says Brent's mom, Lorene, in her grainy deep voice.

"Look what I found!" I hold up a beautiful sea shell. With the next sea wave, I rinse it off.

"Let me see," says Brent. He grabs it out of my hand and takes off running across the beach. We climb up the steps of the sea wall and hurry across Seawall Boulevard, to show our parents the treasure we found. Brent is not much taller than I am, but he is faster. He runs on ahead of me shouting with excitement and leaving me behind! When I arrive, I see Brent, quietly sneaking out of a cabin.

"That's not our cabin!" His eyes are as big as

saucers and his face is blood red.

"What did you see?" I ask.

"Aw, nothing," he mumbles. He is very embarrassed. *I have always wondered what he saw.*

With summer over it is back to school. Grade school, middle school and high school, are all located in the same large building. There is another school for black kids. Texas schools are segregated.

My sister is five grades above me. She and Brent's sister, Vicki, left a legacy of being one of the smartest classes ever in Winona school. This leaves Brent and me with a cloud hanging over us. Every teacher compares us to our sisters and they expect us to perform accordingly! Vicki graduates as valedictorian and Perry is the class salutatorian.

Brent and I maintain decent grades. In junior high and high school, my primary focus is the social aspect of life!

In 1958, at the age of thirteen, I am old enough to take driver's education and I get my driver license! I still have to walk to school. We have one car so my big driving experience is on rare occasions driving around our small town.

"OK," says Daddy. "You can drive one mile by yourself." What did I do? I backed the car all over Winona! Miles do not add up when you are in reverse! Maybe that is why I can back up so well as an adult!

"W! H! S!" I am a cheerleader in junior high and later high school. I have to maintain passing grades to continue cheerleading, so I make them, only for that reason.

The annual social high school highlight is the Junior Senior Banquet. Freshmen and sophomores are drilled with, "You can't go until you are at least a junior."

I nervously wait for an answer.

Finally, "Hello," comes from at the other end of the phone line.

"Ronnie? This is Suzie. I realize this is short notice but my plans for the Junior Senior Banquet have flopped. Is there any chance you can go with me to the banquet tomorrow night?"

"Sure Suzie, what time?"

Ronnie has come to my rescue. The life of a teen is full of drama. This is one example of the trauma and uncertainty, which is major in the daily life of a teen.

The banquet is lovely and Ronnie looks great. He is my knight in shining armor. "Such a lovely couple," I hear several times. Can you imagine the horror and shame of a fifteen-year-old cheerleader not having a date for the banquet?

Drama indeed! Ronnie Applewhite stepped up to the plate.

Although my friends and I are crazy, I am not boy crazy. I date very little and enjoy hanging out with the high school gang. Flirting with athletes of the opposing teams is a cheerleader's favorite thing to do.

My friend, Beth, is dating a Big Sandy boy named Clifford. Big Sandy is eight miles down the road and our biggest football rival.

"Come on Suzie. Can we make it a double date?" Beth asks.

"It's not just a double date, it is a blind date for me!" I am a high school sophomore and not even interested in going steady with anyone.

"He is an athletic star from Big Sandy. He plays football, basketball and his high school jacket is covered with track metals," exclaims Beth.

Not only is he muscular, he is big! I weigh eighty-six pounds, barely five feet tall. My date, Roy Eudy, is five feet ten inches and a hundred and ninety pounds.

Chapter 2
Love At First Sight?

Was it love at first sight? Clifford seemed to think so! He laughed and said that after our blind date, Roy rode down the road with his head sticking out the window shouting, "I'm in love and I love Suzie!" Needless to say, that was all I needed to hear. Roy and I went steady for the continuation of that school year.

We kept Mother on her toes. She was always waiting to make sure I was in the house by eleven on weekdays and midnight on weekends. Many times, she would open the front door around the eleven o'clock hour and find us out in the street. Roy would be holding me over his head and spinning around, his arms stretched straight up over his head with me stretched out like Superwoman flying-lying stiff, toes pointed one way and hands reaching the other, my tummy riding on his two big hands.

"You're going to get run over!" Mother would yell. You could tell she was irritated; the catch was to see how many times we could go round and round, shouting and laughing. When we were dizzy enough, we would tumble onto the front yard, careful to miss the barrel cactus Daddy had planted. In spite of the fun, we would have to be in the house by Mother's curfew.

"Let's get married!" It was April. I was a junior in high school. Roy was completing his first year of college. We boldly went to my parents and expressed our desires!

"We will think about it," Mother said. Daddy was the head of our family, and he had Mother's permission to say so. He was a hard worker and was gone much of the time. When mother said "We" there may be a discussion, but she would be the final judge.

The next day we went back for the verdict.

"You know this is NOT what we want. But, if you insist on getting married we'll consent," we wiggled and squirmed with excitement when we hugged.

"Hold on!" Mother stopped us. "That is only if you will agree to our stipulations!" Mother began her speech. "You are in love, and love makes us do things we would not ordinarily do. Like get married at your age. My first stipulation is: you will graduate from high school."

My parents always had a "start-to-finish" attitude. When you start something, you have to finish it. To them education separated the successful people from the failures.

"Marriage is a big step in life," she continued, "and you should do it because you want to and not because you have to." Mother knew a couple of the girls in high school got pregnant. Although she never said it, she thought I could end up being another one of "those pregnant girls." The choices seemed to be sex, pregnancy, or teenage marriage.

"When you have children everything changes. You must not have children for five years. We will go to Doctor Bradford for a counseling session." The doctor's appointment was to inform me about the birds and the bees, plus to advise me on birth control.

There was no "pill" and I already knew about the birds and the bees. I learned this information from dirty jokes while riding to football games on the school bus.

Mother really did not have anything to worry about. I was a virgin. Under no circumstances, would I have agreed to sexual promiscuity. Even Roy agreed to this. Sex, however, was one reason we wanted to get married!

We were in love and we had a wonderful compatible relationship.

We set the date for June 1, 1962! In a jewelry store window, I found a beautiful half-carat diamond ring with fifteen small diamonds surrounding the large stone.

"I don't understand why you want such an expensive ring," said Mr. Eudy, my future father-in-law. "But I'll co-sign if you want to buy it on credit."

As a bride to be, I was treated special by everyone. A huge shower was planned for me at Margie Dale's.

I felt honored selecting china, crystal, and silver. Selections were made at several department stores! I did not realize this was a part of the marriage scene, but I went along with it and marveled.

The wedding shower was amazing! There were many wonderful gifts. I had no idea people cared so much for Roy and me. Their acts of kindness touched my heart! Everyone was treating me like a princess and I felt the respect. Inside, I knew they were not glad that I was marrying so young.

Mother informed me that a bride should have a bridal trousseau, something special to wear for the honeymoon. This sounded great, so we went to Tyler on a shopping spree! It was a little bit strange because the two of us ended up in the children's clothing department. I was young and very small. Sexy negligees and nightgowns looked like oversized baggy hand-me-downs. None of the clothes in the women department could be cut down to "Suzie size." Therefore, to the children's department we went!

June 1, 1962, was the wedding date at my Methodist

Church in Winona. I was a young girl fulfilling a big dream. I found the love of my life at this early age. Everyone seemed happy for me and we were ready to begin a new chapter in our lives! Not only were we going to be one, we knew that we were both, one in Christ.

WE ARE ONE

Life is lived from day to day –
And daily His will be done,
Our mortal lives in the flesh
Have strength drawn from the Son.

Our praise continues forever I see
God manifesting Himself through you and me!
His word is light, His word is true!
I am His Lamb and so are you!

As sheep we always depend on God.
Our Shepherd, He remains for sure.
Thank God, He cares and loves us so,
It's His love that makes us pure!

Under God's wing, I stand amazed.
The protection He gives so free.
It's simple, easy, and wonderfully good,
I wonder why all can't see!!!
                    Suzie

Chapter 3
Marriage To Roy

What a big day in our lives! Me, weighing 86 pounds, a girl almost seventeen years old and big strong 189 pound Roy, a young man at nineteen. We were ready to begin a new chapter in our lives and were excited to assume our rolls in marriage. We were truly in love, having eyes only for one another. Both of us knew God and agreed to be dependent on Him throughout our marriage.

The Methodist church began to fill up for the early afternoon June wedding. Family and friends joined in the celebration as we said our vows. I wore a pretty calf length gown, which was loaned to me by the pastor's wife. The altar was adorned with gorgeous red, pink and white roses. Daddy walked me down the aisle and gave me away. The small wedding was perfect as we two youngsters dared to begin life as husband and wife.

The Methodist Church has three sets of pews, two short sets on the outside and the long set in the middle. Sister Perry Jo brought her family from Abilene. Mother, along with mostly McClennys sat on my side of the church while Roy's parents, his sister, Nancy, with her husband, Charles, along with a few others sat on his side. Soon the middle filled with our friends.

Everyone was happy to watch us tie the knot. Well almost everyone. My nine-year-old brother cried all during the ceremony.

"Everyone thought how sweet it was. How I was so upset that my sister was leaving home!" Mitch still tells the story. "I didn't care if she got married and left home. I was crying because she squished my cat! She backed over

Flossy and killed her, right in front of me. She, in her fancy clothes, on her way to the church left my cat flip-flopping right in the driveway!"

We planned a one o'clock wedding in order for us newlyweds to complete a five-hour drive to our honeymoon reservation. A quick reception gave enough time for friends to decorate the car. A fast change of clothes and we were off, on schedule. Where else? We were Galveston bound!

"We had a beautiful wedding, everything was perfect and everything went as planned!" I said so excitedly.

"And now we're on our own," said Roy.

"Yes, we are, finally, on our way to Galveston. In five hours we will be there."

"Five hours! Whose idea was this?" ask Roy, "We are newlyweds you know!"

"Well, we made the plans!" I answered. "Since we made 'em, we can surely break 'em!"

As a happy couple, we began looking for a suitable motel in the next city! In Rusk, a long one hour drive from Winona, we bedded down for the night and there we made history! For years, a private joke between us was relating back to our first "adult decision". We decided it had been a good one.

The next day we were honeymooning in Galveston. For four days, I enjoyed showing Roy highlights of the city. As we passed the notorious Hotel Galvez, I explained this was where my parents honeymooned. We laughed, loved, and knew we were blessed.

Our lives were not as well planned as our honeymoon. There were only two things certain. Roy had a good paying summer job with an oil company and our Gladewater apartment rent was paid for at least a month. The two of us also knew there would be a car payment of $90.00 a month and a ring payment of $10.00 a week! With this, we felt secure and saw no problems ahead. Our belief was, with God and with love, we could conquer anything that might get in our way.

The honeymoon ended, the marriage was strong. Life was fun and we lived as though our joy would never end.   Roy was a funny person.   He had his times of depression and sudden mood changes, but he kept me laughing most of the time. We socialized with friends on weekends.

His good summer job with Sun Oil Company ended in September. First hurdle for us was a realization that we needed more than love to survive. First and foremost, we realized our need to call on the name of Jesus! That we did and amazingly, a job fell into Roy's lap! Even while dating, we had been a praying couple, and, we decided that prayer should always be a big part of our lives. Roy went to work for the Texas Highway Department in their field office. He loved the work but it paid little. At least it was a job. Now we would have to learn to manage our money.

We saved enough money for Roy to continue his education by taking night courses at Tyler Junior College. I began my night studies at John Tyler high school fulfilling my conditions of finishing high school. I only needed three credits to graduate, so one semester of night classes was perfect.

Roy's new job was in Tyler.   We moved from Big Sandy to Tyler, fifteen miles from Winona.   We needed more money so I went to work for Skillern's Drug Store as a clerk. Not long after, I became pharmacist's assistant and began making the daily financial reports in the office.

I had just come back from lunch and was working in that small office, listening to the radio. A popular song of the day, *Washington Square*, came on. I had heard hundreds, if not thousands of songs on the radio and it was not unusual to hear that song. I remember that particular song because it was playing, just after noon, on November 22, 1963. The end of the song was cut off and replaced with an unusual silence. "Dead air," they call it. Then a crackle was followed by the voice of Walter Cronkite.

"Breaking News! President Kennedy…has just been shot…in downtown Dallas…this afternoon at 12:30!"

Everyone was shocked. The news was traveling across the airways on radio and television! No one could believe, or wanted to believe what they heard! Our young president, the man we had grown to admire and love, John F. Kennedy was shot! Even "America's Anchorman" Walter Cronkite, lost his composure.

"The president…is dead."

If you heard those words, you remember where you were and what you were doing. Forty-six years later, o*n September 11 we again experienced that shocked silence that swept across the United States.*

President John F. Kennedy was a young forty-six-year-old and had been in office for almost three years. He was the thirty-fifth president of The United States of America. His election was controversial. President Kennedy was very handsome and the youngest man ever to be elected president. He was the first Catholic president. He was treated like a movie star and idolized by the press and public.

By 1:40 pm, only seventy minutes after the assignation, the culprit, Lee Harvey Oswald had been apprehended! At 2:38 pm, Lyndon Johnson took the oath of office. With Jacquelyn Kennedy at his side, he was sworn in on Air Force one before it departed from Love Field in Dallas. A Texan was our new president!

We had planned a trip after work that fateful day. My sister, Perry, lived in Abilene, Texas with her husband and children.

In 1962, there were very few interstates. And, what was a loop?

The route from Tyler to Abilene went through downtown Dallas, past the location where the shooting took place. Much to our amazement the road was not closed. We were able to drive slowly past the very location where President Kennedy was shot, just hours earlier. We learned from the radio where the shots came from, so we looked up to the sixth floor of the Texas Schoolbook Depository. Many were gathered at Dealey Plaza where the assassination took place. Other than that, nothing appeared unusual.

In today's world, there would be yellow tape and barricades everywhere for days.

Two days later, Oswald was being escorted by police to transfer him from Police Headquarters to Dallas County Jail. He was shot and killed by Jack Ruby, a Dallas Nightclub owner. It all happened live on American television!

Although the events transpired rapidly, it took months for everyone to get over the shock of the terrible tragedy. Most businesses closed the day of the funeral and all eyes were glued to the TV for days. It was a very sad time for American Citizens.

LIGHT IN DARKNESS

Jesus is alive and dwells among us!
How can we praise Him enough?
Abiding right here in the midst of darkness,
How can we praise Him enough?

Our Comfort in times of trial and pain
Our strength when we need it most.
Jesus our Savior; lives forever –
Bringing Light as he saves the lost!

The beam of His presence flutters about.
We rejoice and live with action!
God's love, His will, revealed through us;
Amazing – so Great – Satisfaction!!

The light that glows, a beam coming forth,
Allows us to recognize our brother.
In everyday living, with darkness about,
As Christians, we recognize each other!

The trumpet sounds, every knee shall bow
And every tongue confess His name!
Why wait for the trumpet, why live in the dark?
When His wonders we NOW can proclaim!

Our mission on earth? Bring praise to the Lord!
By God's grace, with hearts pure and clear.
The Father sustains and protects,
As the Spirit leads and directs,
Light in the darkness is here!
      Suzie

Chapter 4
The Good Years

The marriage continued to be a good one. We finished our year of schooling, held down our respective jobs and both realized life was good. We had promised Mother, there would be no children for five years and we were faithful to adhere to the promise. The truth is we were far too busy enjoying life together to mess it up with children!

Unlike today, young ladies planned to get married right after finishing high school and began adulthood with their husband.

Several of my high school friends were married and our social lives flourished. We intertwined with these couples. (Beth & Charles, Brent & Kay, Phil and Lynda) All their marriages have lasted!

Roy's way of doing things was very comical. Everyone enjoyed being around him because his personality was entertaining. He did silly things, and knew his actions would make people laugh. One particular thing was to trim the hedges! Every week he would literally pick up the running gas lawnmower and mow the shrubs flat on the top and sides. Twigs flying, blade spinning, motor roaring we would watch in amazement. It was very dangerous, and he did it just to show his extraordinary strength and to keep us laughing!

The Vietnam War was raging in 1965. Roy was twenty-two years old and I was twenty. Many people disagreed with that war and a large number of people protested it. The military draft was in effect. We knew it was only a matter of time until Roy would be called to duty. If we had a baby it would get him deferred, but that was out of the question because of our promise to Mother.

We were living in Dallas where Roy worked as a drafter for an engineering firm. I was working part time and we lacked for nothing. We acknowledged God's blessings on our lives daily. We were soul mates, though at that time, the expression was not used.

The war continued and a large number of our East Texas boys went to Vietnam. Some were forced and others went because they felt it was their duty. My cousin, Sam Attwood, returned home to spend the remainder of his life in a wheelchair, as a paraplegic. My dear friend Alice Faye Jackson was at home pregnant and praying that her husband would return safely. Most of our friends were blessed to make it back, but like so many other young men, Alice Faye's husband was killed in battle. An impressive Vietnam War Memorial is in the National Mall in Washington, DC. More than once, I have had the privilege to view the name, John Alvie Nicholas, engraved on *The Wall*. (Panel 24W – Line 31) The 58,286 names on the Vietnam Veterans Memorial were soldiers who died in the Vietnam War. I get very sad when I go there.

To end the suspense of waiting for the draft letter from Uncle Sam that starts with "Greetings", Roy volunteered for the U.S. Army. By volunteering, he would only have to serve two years, as opposed to three. Of course, that meant Vietnam was inevitable. With the induction letter, Roy gave notice to his employer. We moved our furniture and everything we owned to Winona. I stayed with my parents, like Mother did, while my husband was serving his country.

Basic training was not easy for Roy. Not easy, is putting it mildly! Roy had a difficult time adjusting to Army life with his personality traits of depression and mood swings. He was a strong athletic person, so physically he was at the top of his class.

We had been inseparable during our three years of marriage. Never in a million years would I have guessed that Roy would not be able to hold up mentally to the pressure of separation!

"Mrs. Eudy," the Sergeant told me on the phone. "Private Eudy is too dependent on you. He is not adjusting at all."

A few days later Roy called, "It's over! I can come home! The Army agreed to issue me an Inadaptable Discharge."

"What?" I exclaimed, "No way! What are you thinking? You cannot do that! Do not agree to anything. I'll be there tomorrow!" That I did.

After a night of praying, I felt confident I was doing the right thing. I drove to Leesville, Louisiana where Roy was in training. I somehow (by God's intervention most likely) received special permission to visit Roy and then gave him a strong lecture.

"You will regret your decision to quit. Unless you persevere in this, you may never regain your self-esteem." Then I let him have it with both barrels. "I am very disappointed in you! Only a couple of months more and I will go with you wherever you go." This was not reality and I knew it.

Roy completed basic training and received orders for his next training class. The orders had in bold print "single status". This meant that he was to travel and train alone. He was to report to Presidio of San Francisco, California. Roy and I decided not to let the orders separate us. Together, we loaded our Volkswagen bug to the brim and headed for San Francisco, taking with us towels, wash clothes, pots and pans. We even took my sewing machine. Actually almost everything one would need to run a small household was in that little car!

Roy had never been out of Texas. I had barely been out of Texas, so the journey to San Francisco, California was scary! There was no GPS. We laughed and confessed our faith, with the confidence that God was directing us, as He had so many times before. Day after day the packed up little faded blue "Beatle" or "Slug Bug" rolled on and on. There was so much land! We had no idea it was so far across the United States and felt more homesick with each mile that passed by.

We crossed New Mexico then on to Arizona, the miles clicked by.

With the sun going down, we crossed the Nevada state line and pulled into a small motel. It was nothing fancy and looked to be reasonably priced. I was the designated "money carrier" for this trip and began reaching for the stash. (*In the 1960s, credit cards, ATMs, even checking accounts were not often used.*) We left Texas with a few Travelers Checks and $364.00 in cash. All the money we had in the world was safely stored in my wallet, under my control.

"Roy, it isn't in my purse!" I said.

"What?"

"My wallet! The money! It's not here!" I cried. I looked beside the seat, under the seat, on the floorboard, in the tight crack between the back seat and lap seat. It was not there.

I began to backtrack.

I remembered the last stop was at a gas station. I gave Roy a $10.00 bill to pay for the gas. I then went to the bathroom and took only my wallet instead of taking my purse. In slow motion, I distinctly remembered laying the wallet on the edge of the dingy sink in that small rest room. For the life of me, I did not remember picking it up when I left.

Panic began to take over! We took everything out of the front seats of our 1964 Volkswagen. The back seat was packed so full, we knew it would not be there. We looked and looked. My purse was accounted for, but no wallet.

"Where did we stop?" Roy asked.

"I can't remember the name of the little town. It was over a hundred miles back!" I answered. "What are we going to do?"

We went into the motel office. The desk clerk shook his head as we told of our present circumstances. Then he assured us we could go ahead and spend the night.

"Tomorrow things will be better," he said. I wonder how many times that clerk had heard and helped strangers along the way. We must have stopped at the right place.

"You will be in room 14. It is about in the middle of that section. He pointed across the parking lot and handed us the key."

In those days, there were no cell phones, digital maps or internet searches. It was not as simple as picking up a phone and asking your parents for help.

We had been married for three years. We had proven we were independent and able to take care of ourselves. Now we were stuck in the middle of nowhere and flat broke. We were devastated.

Roy and I went into room number 14. I was crying, "It's my fault. I can still see it, the wallet, lying on the sink."

"Babe," affirmed Roy. He put his big arms around me, "it is going to be OK. You know God has miraculously gotten us out of scrapes before. Why can't we trust him to do it this time?"

We prayed fervently. We needed Devine

intervention! There was nothing else to do but trust God.
Suddenly, there was calmness in the room - a peace that
was beyond understanding.

"It is done," declared Roy. "There is nothing else
WE can do." We both dropped off to sleep.

At daybreak, I was up and sneaking out of the room.
I planned to completely empty the car. If the wallet was in
the car, I was going to find it.

I unlocked the car door and I could not believe what
my tear swollen eyes saw! To my amazement, the wallet
was laying wide open there in the middle of the passenger
seat. The wallet, which we had searched for so frantically,
looked as though it had dropped out of the sky!

"Roy! Come! Roy, come on!" He knew something
was up and slipped on a pair of pants. He followed me out
to the car parked right in front of room 14.

We laughed and cried as we realized God had saved
us again. It was truly a miracle. This was a wonderful and
true miracle, which we told many times during the eleven
years of our marriage.

UNBELIEVABLE

Father produces a phenomenon,
We scarce can take it in!
Amazed, excited and thrilled beyond words
It's too much to comprehend!

By his Spirit, God comforts and sooths
With all wisdom, He confirms!
Will we ever cease to be amazed?
To see the way our life is turned.

Can we grow expecting miracles?

It's real, but so farfetched.
This miracle blessed our heart!
We excitedly wait for the next!

I believe God smiles seeing His child
Gasp in wonder and awe!
God in His glory has joy as He gives
So He fills until we overflow!
(That is true! Psalms 23:5)
       Suzie

We arrived in San Francisco, a short wonderful experience. Advanced Individual Training (AIT) in the Army is usually a crash course on how to survive in a particular field. The training is intense and wives are seldom in the picture. In three months, Roy received his orders. We were dreading that day. We were sure, like everyone else in his company, Vietnam would be his destination.

"Report to Baumholder, Germany," his orders said, much to our surprise. We were ecstatic to say the least.

Several months after Roy went to Germany, I was flying crossing the Atlantic Ocean!

We had many memorable times in Germany. We met Bobby and Joyce Bishop, who have remained our lifelong friends. We learned how to make friends, which included anyone who could speak English!

We celebrated our fifth wedding anniversary in Paris, France.

"Well," boasted Roy, "we kept our end of the deal: five years and no kids!"

Five months later, we had a beautiful baby girl! I was twenty-two years old when, on November 24, 1967, Ann Toinette Eudy arrived, weighing nine pounds and twelve ounces! We named her after Queen Marie Antoinette and immediately began calling her Twan.

Roy's military obligation was almost over with his tour of duty in Germany. He was ready to be a regular civilian again.

Back in Texas, we realized not much had changed! There were jobs, but very few were desirable. A dream of Roy's was to work in Longview for a company called Texas Eastman, a division of Kodak. Prior to the Army, there was no chance of getting a job there. Completed military service was almost a requirement for this company. Many veterans were returning home and looking for jobs. We knew it would take a while to be hired. Giving the credit to God, we rejoiced when Roy was hired after his third interview. In Roy's opinion, it was the best job in East Texas with wonderful pay and good benefits. Longview was about 25 miles from Winona, a nice city to raise our family.

We bought a little red brick house in Longview and met some wonderful people. One couple with whom we became good friends was Phillip and Brenda Mann. They had a daughter the same age as Twan and we did many family things together. The times were good, God continued to bless our lives and we were very happy. Good fortune and dreams had come true.

It was the year 1969. The date was July 20. I was 24 years old and I remember it well. Brenda and I drove from Longview to Winona to visit Mother. Twan and Kim, our daughters, had enjoyed the afternoon playing in the country while Mother entertained. Night snuck upon us and the sky was dark when we drove away from Mother's house.

Listening to the radio, we realized Neil Armstrong was making his much-anticipated moonwalk from Apollo

11! We immediately stopped the car, turned the radio up and got out. A full moon was visible. It shone brightly and we felt as though we could literally see Armstrong on the surface of it! Of course, that was our immigrations running wild!

The radio went silent and then began to make a crackling sound; a voice came all the way from the moon. "That's one small step for man, one giant leap for mankind." We were so excited as we stood outside gazing at the moon like millions of other people. We stood there for a long time. When we got back in the car, Twan and Kim were both sound asleep. Little did they care that history was made that night.

About this time, Roy's older brother, Jack, had a great job working for an oil company. He had a pontoon boat, fishing boat, nice automobiles, and everything a Texas man would want. With a wife and two children (ages 9 and 13) he was the ideal "Family Man". From out of nowhere, he left his wife and family! We were surprised and devastated. Jack had always been the model father and husband. Suddenly, he no longer cared for the kids or his wife, Betty. He walked out, leaving Betty to support the family.

The world moved on. Betty worked and raised the children. The children continued their lives, fatherless, and had emotional problems. Terry, their beautiful daughter seemed to be getting it together, becoming an Airline Stewardess, only to commit suicide while in her twenties. I lost track of Bubba the younger son and eventually Betty remarried.

Six months after Jack left, his other brother, Horace, did the same thing. Yes, both brothers abandoned their families.

These events disturbed Roy greatly! Being a sensitive, moody and deep thinking person, he would often reflect on these events.

"They walked out. I wonder, I will do the same?" Roy would ask this from time to time.

I always made a silly face and asked, "Why do you think you would ever do that?" We never really dealt with it.

The job with Texas Eastman was everything Roy thought it would be. He loved being a chemical operator. We were living our American dream. Twan was just over two years old and growing up in our nice little home. We were very content. ,

"Mama is going to have a baby. You are going to have a little brother or sister!" I explained to her. We were happy to expand the family!

In November, 1970, Twan became three and I turned twenty-five. On November 4, 1970, Connie Lynn Eudy was born in Longview, Texas, weighing in at nine pounds and seven ounces. Connie brought so much joy into our home! *I had many home movies, but they are long gone, lost over the years.* Our friends, Phillip and Brenda, had another daughter about the same time we had Connie. It was a great time in our lives.

"All I want in life are a few acres, out in the middle of nowhere, to farm and raise my family. A family is not complete without a son," Roy would comment.

We found eight acres for sale a few miles out of Winona. As a Texas Veteran, Roy was able to get a VA loan and we bought the land with a small down payment. The monthly payments were scattered over many years!

Marv, Perry Jo's husband, told us about a little house that was for sale, to be moved. The house was a six thousand dollar model home! *Houses that size were selling for around twelve thousand at that time.* With a bank loan we began our dream toward farm living. We had a house in one place and land in another.

There was NO road to the land we bought! We had to go across someone else's land to get to our eight acres. It was landlocked! Road easements had to be obtained before a road could be built. Power lines had to be strung across the countryside so we could have electricity.

A septic tank and field lines had to be dug.

"The big problem is water. Where could we get water?"

We called a "water witch", John Wyman. The local old-timer was famous for locating exactly where water would be found and could tell how deep the well would have to be.

With a Y shaped willow branch, he walked around the property for thirty minutes the Y pointing to the direction he needed to go. Every now and then, he would stop and turn around in a circle. Then he would walk again.

At one point, he stopped and the willow branch bent to the ground. He scraped an X to mark the spot with the heel of his cowboy boot.

"Forty-two feet deep," he said.

Roy asked, "How much do we owe you?"

"How much water do you want?"

Roy gave him eight dollars, which was all he had on him.

We drilled right where he said and thirty-five feet deep, but no water was to be found. The drilling crew left us with a dry hole, forty-six feet deep and three feet across.

Starr Mountain Community water ran along the county road, a half a mile away. With a few more miracles, and with God's help, we were able to have a rough road built and water lines installed all the way to our little "farmhouse dream" in the middle of nowhere!

When we went to fill the "dry hole", we discovered the well was full of water! Water literally came to the top of the ground. Old-timer, John Wyman, was good at his calling. We knew water was always where John predicted!

On Roy's days off, we built a one-room shack on the farm. The four of us loved "going to the farm" and stayed there every chance we had. Roy was scheduled to be off five days in a row every month. Twan was four and Connie was just starting to toddle.

"Let's go to the farm. I want to go to the farm," Twan would beg. We were at our home in Longview. Twan and Roy were a team. Sometimes they would ride the motorcycle to the farm to work. Connie and I found other things to do.

Finally, the road was improved to our land, the electric lines were installed and the house we bought was moved onto the property! It was a joyous day when we sold the property in Longview and moved all of our belongings to the farm.

Texas Eastman was in Gregg County, thirty-five miles from our house. We lived in Smith County. Being a chemical operator required rotating shift work.

"God did not intend for people to work all night. Night is for sleep, not for work," Roy often said.

Roy would get depressed before working all night

on the graveyard shift. He weighed this against his job as our livelihood and all benefits of working for a big corporation.

We joined the Winona First Baptist Church and attended it consistently. It was a good church and we met old friends and made new ones. Roy was raised a staunch Baptist and I dutifully followed.

We were living in the same area as my family and I became very close to my sister and her family. On weekends, we usually went to Perry Jo's house and played cards. It was common for friends and neighbors to join us.

We fenced the property and purchased a goat and a couple of Basset Hounds. We planned to raise and sale long eared puppy dogs.

After a few months of country living, we decided to have another child!

"Let it be a boy!" Roy prayed for the third time. Prayer did not work the first or second time. Again, he was hoping for a boy.

Roy borrowed a tractor and plowed a garden. We planted onions, tomatoes, squash, potatoes and beets.

Roy also mowed with the tractor. There was the large field in front of the house. As he was mowing one day, I saw Roy driving down and around the field on the tractor with his arms flying high. Sometimes he would stand up, hands waving and pointing, as the tractor rolled on. I could tell he was well engrossed with something.

"What in the world were you doing out there?" I asked. I have never seen such a grin and smile on his face. "Why are you so happy?"

"I am happy, extremely happy! I love owning and working my own land. I love my family. I love being off work. I have so much love I had to PREACH OUT to the hills the fields and the clear blue sky!"

SUCH POWER

The greatness of Gods power
Lives in us today!
As we live our life in Jesus
He is the only way!

I shudder when I realize
The power in our hands!
Only can a true living God
Give such power to mere man!

God reigns over the universe
Using you and me.
We praise His Holy Greatness
Through us, may the whole world see!

Suzie

Chapter 5
Troubled Waters

During our eleventh year of marriage, I gained a lot of weight. Seven months pregnant, and I felt my figure was less than desirable. The other babies looked like a bump on a stick. This time I looked like a big fat log.

"The guys at work say I should have an affair;" said Roy. "Especially, since I am only a one-woman man. They say I don't know what I'm missing." This bothered Roy and I noticed his mood swings became more and more frequent.

Twan loved to meet her dad coming home from work. The five-year-old refused to come to the house until Daddy got home. Every day she would wait at the end of the long dusty driveway. She was waiting to see Roy riding in the big green Mercury Marque. His arrival got later and later.

"Come on, Twan. It's getting late and Daddy must be working overtime tonight." I knew something was not right.

"What's over dime? Where is he?"

"Come on. It's getting dark and I have supper ready. We'll see him when he comes home."

Connie was almost three years old and happy with the thought of having a new baby in the house. *(At that time there was no way to tell what the gender of a baby would be—except for the pencil on a string method and a few other superstitions designed to try!)*

At the age of twenty-seven, the contractions started and I was in labor. Roy took me to Good Shepherd Hospital in Longview. On April 2, 1973, we had a beautiful nine pound three ounce baby boy! He was the smallest of my big birth children. We named him Roy Jerome Eudy! Yes! We finally had a boy to complete our family.

HE IS ALL

The magnitude of God's love for me
Is a far greater thing than I can see.
It exceeds all my finite mind can take.
Yet, because of God's love, Perfection is made!

Through us, Perfection shall be exemplified.
As our lives he cleanses and purifies.
We live to do the will of God
As every day, this path we trod!

No big deal, just everyday living
As strength He is continually giving.
Our life shall be one of glory for Him
His light shines through; it will never grow dim!

We now have this boy,
We thank you so much,
Each day of his life
May he feel your touch!

Thank you Lord for our beautiful son!
    Suzie

After the big event, the birth of a son, Roy drove home from the hospital to clean up. It would be the last time I saw him as a devoted husband and father.

On his way back to visit us, Roy decided to celebrate by stopping at a honky-tonk (beer joint) in Gladewater. Gladewater is on the way to Longview, where Jerome and I were waiting at the hospital.

In Texas, beer and liquor are not sold just anywhere. In the 1900's there were many counties which forbade the sale of alcoholic beverages. Smith County was "dry" and certainly did not allow the sale of such!

Roy dressed up, climbed into his big nice car and headed for Gregg County. With a feeling of celebration and the prodding to be promiscuous from his co-workers, Roy drove across the county line. Looming in the back of his mind were the actions of his two brothers. The gravel made a crunching noise as he parked alongside old and new pickups and cars. He walked toward the dingy gray building with its cracked and peeling paint. He stepped through the swinging doors and into the darkness of "The Green Frog."

I was released from the hospital and Roy drove us to Starrville to pick up the kids. Twan and Connie were staying with my mother. Roy seemed overjoyed about having a son. He rejoiced on the outside, but there was a cloud on the inside.

I was happy to get back to our farm. I knew life would be different with a newborn and expected some changes. We were all back home, but we were not the happy family I remembered or imagined. Two days after Jerome and I got home, Roy began to stay away more and more.

"Suzie, I met someone," Roy told me, his head bowed as if he were ashamed. However, there was the sound of conviction in his voice. Right or wrong, he had made his decision. "Her name is Georgia. She's a gypsy and lives out of her pick-up truck."

I sat there, so shocked I could not say anything. All I could do was breathe while Roy told his story.

"I went into the bar to celebrate Jerome's birth and sat down beside her. She has beautiful, long red hair, nice figure, and she smelled good," he said. "By the time I had finished a couple of beers, I knew her life story. Suzie, it's a sad story," he continued. "She has been a victim in so many ways."

Roy was talking to me as though I should be sympathetic and understanding. I felt like I was the victim here. I was still in shock and he went on.

"Georgia told me I reminded her of her deceased brother. She was so close to him, which made her feel very close to me."

If you personally knew Roy, you might be able to understand how he would be affected by this story. She gained his sympathy. Roy hungered to be needed and wanted. Georgia fulfilled all his desires.

In the daylight, Georgia's red hair showed a little gray at the roots. She was slim, maybe too slim. She wore heavy makeup but you could still see she was fifteen years older than Roy was. None of this made any difference. She looked beautiful to him. He had totally fallen for Georgia.

For some reason he felt no obligation to our family, his own family. I was most assuredly upset.

"Just have an affair! I will not tell anyone. One day this infatuation will be over," I begged.

Roy would not hear of that. "It wouldn't be fair to you and the kids. My brothers started this pattern and it is time that I follow in their foot-steps!"

"That makes no sense to me at all," and *IT STILL*

DOES NOT!

One night, Roy came home late to get his clothes. We had a talk which turned into a screaming argument.

"I'm moving out! Georgia and I are renting an apartment and we are moving in together. You can have the car and the old pick-up. I'm taking my clothes and the motorcycle."

"I love you!"

"Suzie! I don't love you. I never loved you. I can't stand to be around you." Roy calmly said. This hurt me immensely.

"Well, thanks for the car. What about the car payments? How are we going to live?" I yelled.

Our shouts woke Twan up. She came wandering into the little kitchen rubbing her eyes. When she saw Roy, she was so happy!

"Daddy!" she shouted with delight and ran to him. I yelled, pointing at him and then pointing towards her.

"You tell her! You tell her you're leaving us."

Roy did exactly that. With his muscular arms, he grabbed her up. These same two muscular arms had playfully thrown her up high in the air, and she would laugh and scream with delight. This time he held her straight out in front of him, like he was going to shake her. It was scary. This was a very different Roy than we had ever known. They looked straight into each other's eyes.

Sternly he said, "I'm leaving, I don't love you anymore, I'm not going to live here anymore." There was anger and hate in his voice. Of course, this upset Twan and she still remembers when her daddy said, "I don't love you."

She was five years old and she thought he was mad at her because she had come into the kitchen. For many years she blamed herself, thinking her dad left home because he was mad at her. Twan was heartbroken and it left a huge scar on her heart.

Roy tried to come back several times after that, but he would only stay for a few days. He was acting strangely, and I didn't feel comfortable with him. I did not trust him at all.

Roy would return to the farm periodically to get more of his clothes. Each meeting was a strain on all of us. My mind was jumping all over the place. I thought maybe if I left the farm this whole situation would miraculously go away.

We had a little money in the bank. I decided to get out of town, at least for a while. My rational was: when Roy returned home and the children and I were gone, the shock factor would jump in. If you remember, this is the same man who tried to get out of the army because of his dependence on me.

I packed our bags to leave. Mitch and his wife Fae lived in North Carolina, stationed in the army. What was I thinking? I loaded up three children, ages five, three, and a baby to drive half-way across the United States! I was in survival mode.

As I drove away from the farm, I was deeply hoping that when I returned, this nightmare would be over. The plan: Roy would come home, realize his mistake and the family would be safe and sound, together again. I knew Roy; I was actually confident this would happen.

I left him a note on the kitchen table:

I am getting the hell out of Dodge. You can stay here, but don't bring that slut into my house. Get over her! I just want us to get back

to where we were and you need to get your head out of your.....
Feed the dogs.

OK, that was the note my editor wrote. This is the note I wrote.

Roy,
Can't believe what is happening. I decided to leave for a while and give you a chance to get your mind straight! Don't know when I'll be back.
The kids and I love you and will miss you.

Pick the vegetables and feed the dogs.

We had a few farm animals and I made sure they were fed. The dogs were in a nice pen and I filled up their water pans and gave them enough food for a couple of days. I trusted that when Roy came back and read the note, especially mentioning the dogs, he would stay home and take over all the animal care.

I drove to Winona and stopped at the Winona Texaco Station. Mother and Daddy owned and operated the gas station. With tears in my eyes, I told them the devastating news. This was the first they had heard of my situation. They could not believe Roy's behavior had changed, seemingly overnight. In the weeks to come, everybody who knew him was shocked as well.

"I have got to go somewhere for a week or so. I'm going to North Carolina to see Mitch and Fae."

"Honey we will be praying for you. Be careful. It may seem like a terrible time now, but it will get better.

Let us know where you are and if you need anything," Mother said.

"I will," I agreed starting the motor. "I think I have everything I need and I'm ready to go."

"Love you!" Mother said, as I put the car in drive.

Before I stepped on the gas, I realized something.

"Daddy," I added, "I don't know where I'm going, and I don't know how to get there!" I just wanted to get away as far and as fast as I could.

"Get on Interstate 20 East and go. Drive for a couple of days. You will know it when you get there," Daddy said.

He wrote down my brother's address.

"They don't even know I'm coming." *(This was before easy communication, no worldwide web and no cell phones!)*

As the kids and I drove away from the station, I saw my parents in the rear view mirror, standing, waving and (while in shock), praying for a safe trip and a safe return of their daughter and grandkids.

The ramp on to Interstate 20 is less than five miles from Winona. I remembered Daddy saying to get on it and just drive! That is exactly what I did! It seemed as though I was the only car traveling the four lanes of concrete. I drove for several hours before I realized I was on Interstate 20 West, going in the opposite direction I should have been driving! Instead of going east, I was passing Dallas, westward bound and headed toward Fort Worth!

As so many times in my life, what looked like the wrong direction turned out to be the right direction! I was nearing Fort Worth by the time I fully grasped the mistake I had made. The sky was turning dark and the lights of the big city were coming on. I mulled over what I thought was a mistake; I realized that God had sent me in that direction.

"It wasn't a mistake after all!" I mumbled to three kids who just looked at me. I could stop for the night at my dear friends, Bobby and Joyce. I knew them from Germany. They now live in Fort Worth!

"Maybe you have some words of wisdom?" I asked Joyce. "I need some time to get a grip on myself. In the morning, I can start my journey over. This time I will start fresh with a plan, and I will know exactly where I'm going." I was beginning to realize this would be a long hard trip! A one-month-old baby demands a lot of attention. Here I was, five hours down the road and in the wrong direction!

As always, Bobby and Joyce were happy to see me. They loved Roy so much and could not believe what happened. Bobby and Joyce had nurtured me in Germany while I was pregnant with Twan. They took me to the hospital and brought us home. As always, we reminisced about the old gang back in Germany. We remembered stories of Roy's comical behavior. They asked if there was anything they could do and I sadly said, "No."

Then, I told them, "I was supposed to go east and I went west. Now, I'm not so sure I can make it by myself. It is so hard to travel with the kids!"

"Great", Joyce exclaimed, "I'll go with you!"

Unknown to me, Joyce's sister and her husband lived in North Carolina. He was stationed at Ft. Bragg, the same place Mitch was!

"There's nothing stopping me," she said. "We can leave in the morning!"

God does answer our need! My mistake was turned into blessing. Joyce is an uplifting person. We tackled that trip with a positive attitude, and Joyce was the best medicine for me. She drove some, took care of the kids some, but most of all, she motivated me. I gained a better outlook on my situation. The trip gave my mind a rest from what was waiting back home. It gave me time to plan for the worst, and hope for the best.

THIS SHIP HE CONTROLS

Leave Him alone,
Why interfere?
God needs no help,
He knows how to steer!

Give Him the rudder
This ship He will guide,
On waves set before us
Smooth ride on the tide!

When the turmoil breaks
On the wind-tossed sea,
God's comfort is offered
Freely to me!

His strength is given
Victory at last!
God needs no help
He always stands fast!
     Suzie

For two weeks I traveled, visited, and prayed. What I really did was run away. I remained optimistic; my upside down life was going to be right side up when I got back to the farm.

The victory I was hoping for turned into disaster. Roy had returned to the house as expected. He packed a few clothes and left. I found the note where I had left it, torn to pieces.

The dogs were skin and bones, almost dead from starvation. The vegetables in the garden were rotting on the vine. Weeds in the yard made the house look abandoned. The house appeared empty, as if whoever had lived there had just walked away.

The dogs survived. My mother-in-law, Alta, worked with dogs, and was able to revive them.

While this broke my heart, there was not a lot of time for self-pity. Roy had brought home good paychecks and we managed very well. When things were good, we had more than we really needed. Now, I was a single mother of three with no paycheck.

A few weeks before this stuff hit the fan my sister, Perry Jo, and I had talked about how totally happy we were. We spoke about how we had both reached a place in our lives where we were content. We could not think of anything more that we needed or even wanted. Perry and I thought our lives would be smooth sailing forever, in our state of bliss. Little did we know what the future would hold! In a moment, in the twinkle of an eye, the road of life can make a drastic turn.

My upheaval came through divorce.

During the eleven years we were married, I had only worked a short time at Skillern's Drug Store, and that was a long time ago. Obviously, I had to get a job. Obviously, I needed to seek childcare. Obviously, I could not stay secluded on that isolated farm. We didn't even have a phone! What was I to do?

I sought God! I had no choice but to rely on Him. I knew God's continual presence and His desire to guide me. If I would keep my eyes on Him, He would surely lead. God did lead, and he did it well!

Why do we wait until there is no other salvation, before we can totally depend on God? Then, when we have lived the miracle, others cannot understand why or how our faith is stronger.

"Never pray for patience," Mother always insisted. "Patience comes with trials and tribulations!"

One of the things God revealed to me was that God is love. I would have to forgive those who had hurt me and even accept some of the blame myself.

Georgia and Roy stayed together. I saw her three times. Each time, I embraced Georgia and told the two of them, "I wish you happiness."

The Accident
Part 2
Cleo and Buffy's View

"Quiet," said Cleo. She gives a stern look to her daughter Buffy There were other words Ron said, but Cleo could not understand them. Cleo looks up to the man; it is six feet from her eyes to his. She has long blond hair. She is a Pekingese.

"Why?" asks her daughter, Buffy. They speak in a language that only dogs can understand.

"You know the drill," remarks Cleo. "The master and the miss do not want to disturb or bother anyone so we sneak out in the middle of the night."

"We are going home?" asks Buffy. Home could be anywhere. Everywhere they go it seems they call it home.

"Home is where they hang the leash," says Cleo.

"Ic zebf hush," said Ron.

"See you got us in trouble again!" barks Cleo.

Both scamper out the front door and run to the Dodge Caravan parked in the grass close by. They are excited and love to ride. With tails wagging, they wait for the side door to open. When it does Buffy leaps in first, trying to outdo her mother.

"What the heck?" she squeals as she falls back out and rolls over. Cleo steps back and looks alarmed. The minivan is full of stuff.

Buffy usually has full roam of the back of the caravan. Tonight the back seats are full of books, luggage, and strange glass things, plastic things, wooden things - all kinds of things. A doggie bed is sitting on top of a cardboard box. It is the only decent place left for them to sit.

With help from Ron, they both make it into the doggie bed.

"This is going to be a long trip," clams Cleo. "There's a lot of stuff in this car." Cleo has learned to estimate how long the trip will be by the amount of luggage and stuff in the car. The more stuff the further and longer they will be gone.

"We must be going to Heaven," suggest Buffy. It is a joke between a mother and daughter. Heaven is a word they use for a long way off. They have traveled very many miles, but they have never been to Heaven. Ron and Elizabeth talk about Heaven and people who have gone there. Sometimes Elizabeth reads about Heaven, from one of her big books, while they are driving down the road. God and Jesus, whoever they are, live in Heaven. Still, after driving thousands of miles, (over eight years for Cleo and six years for Buffy) they have never traveled to Heaven.

The Caravan bounces and turns as it goes across a grassy area and with one big bump, they are on the smooth road again.

Soon Cleo feels the swerve of the van go left and right.

"That's the way the road feels before it straightens out for a long time," reports Cleo. "I think we are on the freeway. I have to go to work." She climbs out of the doggie bed. Then she hops between the front seats and bounces into Master's lap. Her job is to sit in his lap and keep him alert. Occasionally, she will rise up and look out the window, or stick her nose into the blowing air vent and then lie back down so Ron can scratch her behind the ears. "It's a tough job but somebody has to do it."

Buffy stays in the doggie bed. She has tried to sit in Elizabeth's lap but there is always a book or something in the way.   Often Missus will look at a book or some electronic thing and start talking (reading).   Buffy only knows people words she often hears.   Elizabeth talks a lot about Jesus, God and Heaven as the miles go by.

"Have you noticed that when people go to Heaven they don't come back," barks Buffy.
"It must be a gated community," Cleo replies.

Chapter 6
Single Life With Three Children

Although, my family helped me, I felt the need to make it on my own. Roy's parents kept the kids for a week, while I looked for employment. God provided a job immediately! Mother and Perry watched the kids the first few weeks while I worked. Finally, I had saved enough money to move away from that God-forsaken farm.

I was not planning my future. I was concentrating on surviving!

Making land payments was out of the question. I had to unload it somehow. God sent a buyer. Peter Tkach wanted the eight acres of land, but he did not want the house. He was willing to rent the house, until he could build his own. Then I would have to move it.

The sale of the farm got me out from under that debt. Most of the selling price went to the mortgage company to pay the balance on the land. Now I could breathe, knowing the property would not be lost because I could not make payments.

I had a new income. Peter paid rent. This was the first of many times when I would be dealing with houses, rental properties and tenants.

Longview Baptist Temple became my church. My friend, Brenda, helped me with the kids and supported me along with the church. Brenda and another friend, Sherri, became my babysitters while I went to work. They were doing it to help me and it was a little extra money for them. They did not intend for this to be permanent.

I filed for divorce and began receiving $100.00

every two weeks for child support. One Sunday after church, I asked God to direct me in finding a place for us to live in Longview. I had just enough cash to make a deposit on an apartment. The first place I looked was perfect! It was a nice duplex in a residential neighborhood. While looking at the dwelling, I noticed a family across the street. The parents were sitting in their yard on lawn chairs while their two children were playing. I went over and introduced myself to Jenny and Chester Johnson. Before the sun went down that Sunday, God's presence was reaffirmed. If I would seek His guidance, I could live an abundant life!

Jenny agreed to provide day care for all three of my children and starting tomorrow! Jerome was four months old and a wonderful child. Twan and Connie were a handful. They all three loved being at Jenny's and she was the perfect baby sitter.

I moved into the duplex. It was warm and cozy. Early each morning I took the children across the street. Twan recalls that I dressed her on the nights before kindergarten, so all she had to do was wake up and go across the street. Then Jenny gave her breakfast before she caught the bus to school! Later in the day, Jenny would dress Connie and Jerome. I was confident each day they were receiving all the attention and love they needed. What a blessing.

Although I like to think I was the perfect mom, there were several bad mishaps during those trying months. Despite the fact that I had been jilted, I was determined to make sure the kids felt secure. Jerome was so young he didn't know Roy well enough to miss him, but Twan and Connie begged for their dad. I got in touch with Roy and explained their need to see him. We would set a date and time for him to visit, only to experience a no-show. It only took twice for that to happen before I finally wised up. From that time on, I made excuses for Roy, telling the kids that he was too busy working. I made it a point never to say negative things about him and I continued to take the kids to visit with Roy's parents. After all, it wasn't his parents who deserted us. The Eudys were shocked and distraught about Roy's behavior. He almost deserted them as well.

Connie managed to keep me on my toes the most. One weekend I had a chance to work overtime. Jenny only babysat on weekdays. This particular Saturday my friend Sherri agreed to watch them. After a long day of work, I went into Sherrie's house to get the kids. Connie climbed into the car before I came out of the house. Somehow, she managed to pull the gearshift out of park into neutral! The car went down the driveway, across the road, through the bricks and into the kitchen of Sherri's neighbor! What a mess! Fortunately, no one was hurt.

A couple of Saturdays later, the neighborhood kids were playing in Jenny's yard. Connie ran across the street without looking and a Volkswagen bug hit her and knocked her down onto the asphalt

"Mama! Mama!" Twan ran into our house shouting. "Connie got runded over by a car!"

I ran to the porch and stopped. I could not bring myself to go into the road. I stood there on the porch, looking from a distance and crying. In my mind I pictured the worst and I didn't want to see it. An ambulance came and adults were hovering over Connie.

"She's OK," someone finally told me. "A little shook up and bruised, but OK"

The next weekend Twan decided to turn her bicycle

upside down so she could turn the peddles round and round by hand, making the back wheel spin fast in the air. This is what the big kids did. I heard a high pitch scream. I ran to the door and looked out to see blood all over everything! Her finger got caught between the chain and sprocket and cut off the very tip of it. Her finger was bleeding profusely. To the emergency room we went, Twan, her fingertip and me! After analyzing the situation, doctors decided not to put the end back on. They stitched it up, bandaged it nicely and threw her fingertip away. She remembers this every time she looks at her missing fingertip!

I was single, twenty-eight years old with three children under the age of five. I had bills mounting and an ex-husband who did not want to have anything to do with us. I had the responsibility of providing and holding together what was left of our family.

Mother says, "It's through the tough times that a person really gets to know God and His provision. When times are bad a Christian looks to God and is forced to depend on Him for strength and answers."

How true. How true! It is easy to love life, love relationships, love the Church and love God when you are on top of a world of roses. Roy and I had basked in His blessings for years. Now, I was in the valley of roses, without flowers. Roses without flowers are like thorn bushes.

I called on Him in my need. I learned what an awesome God we have! In my state of desperation, I realized I had no strength, no answers, and it required something supernatural to get me through this ordeal!

As I ponder the question in my mind
No simple answer can I find.
Even though we know Him well
Human expressions can't begin to tell,
How enormous, massive and magnificent is He
An explanation of God just cannot be!

WHO IS GOD?

He speaks with a voice,
But no sound is heard.
He's evident in all places,
He's the True Living Word!

As Christians, we see Him,
But the world cannot see.
He shows Himself clearly
It looks impossible to me!

Impossible it is,
For anyone but He.
For the omnipotent God,
The impossible can be!

One more matter I want to present
I want to express how I feel;
I see and hear God, in all that I do,
He is with me and He's so very real!
      Suzie

Chapter 7
Second Marriage
Life with Paul

I am approaching thirty years of age with three children under the age of five. It's no wonder men are not pounding on my door. I am out of practice playing the dating game.

Jenny and Chester encourage me, "Go ahead, get out and have some fun. We will be glad to babysit."

"This is Sig Dickson. He is the principal of Winona Elementary school." Perry Jo introduces me to an "older" gentleman. Perry's husband, Marv, is on the school board and acquainted with Sig. Sig is very nice and he likes me a lot.

We have been dating now for several months. They have been very nice dates including several trips to Dallas. One special night we went to a concert in Shreveport, Louisiana to see Barry Manilow!

A few times now, I have returned home from work and found several beautiful new outfits. Sig borrowed Jenny's key and went into my house. He beautifully displayed the clothing across my bed! How nice is that? After facing an endless struggle with work and these three little ones, to come home to such a surprise!

The dates are fun and we have an understanding that we will be dating each weekend. Still, there seems to be no real commitment. My desire is to find someone to fill the need in my life, someone willing to love me and love my kids. We are a package deal.

"Suzie, Phillip and I have been visiting with a really nice man at the skating rink on Tuesday nights. You know, where we take the kids?" My friend Brenda is excited. "His name is Paul and we've been talking with him and, well, he loves children and he isn't married."

"I'm game," I told Brenda, "Give him my phone number."

He calls me, "Hello, Brenda and Philip told me you were the one for me. I am Paul Murphy. They say you have three kids; I love children!"

Paul tells me about his childhood. He was a baby who was found on the steps of a hospital in Chicago. It was doubtful that Paul would live. He was born without a rectum.

The courts sent him to Omaha, Nebraska, as a ward of a Lutheran Hospital/Home. He lived in the hospital until he was five years old. With his health problems, he was not adoptable. In the daytime he was at the Children's Home, but his permanent room was in the hospital. Lutheran Sisters throughout the complex knew him well and in his words, "I was a very spoiled child."

Paul was a sickly child. He missed many days of school. When he was old enough, he had to do chores. He worked daily in the laundry room. Paul never really had any close friends growing up. Most children who came to the orphanage would soon be adopted.

"It always made me sad to see prospective parents looking for someone to adopt. I knew that it would never be me."

I could feel the pain of rejection in his voice. I know what rejection means.

We spend hours on the phone and know everything we need to know about each other, except, we have never met in person. Is Paul going to change a broken past into a joyful present?

On Sunday, it happens. After church, I introduce Paul to the kids and we go out for lunch. Everything goes well. Paul appears to be an intellectual person. With every subject I mention, he is well informed. We include the kids in our conversations as we get to know one another. We do not have much time for deep conversations. He seems to be very patient with the children and we get along great. He has a good job working as an onsite office manager and an accountant for a large construction firm.

Am I forgetting my troubles and conveniently falling in love? Is this really happening?

I go to bed with him, talking *on the phone* for hours. We begin to spend all of our free time together. The next Sunday, Paul goes to church with me and I take him to Winona to introduce him to my family. The kids love for him to come over. They see me happy and they are happy. Roy's name is heard less and less, since Paul has come into the picture.

"I have a nice double-door refrigerator," Paul mentions, for the third time. "And my furniture is much nicer than yours."

I raise my eyebrows, "He might be the perfect catch!" I pray, "Lord, have you sent him here to love us and help raise the children? He seems generous and has a very giving heart. We were all so heartbroken a few months ago. Thank you Jesus, You have brought someone who has put a smile back on our faces."

"I'm being transferred to New York!" Paul said.

"After only two weeks of dating, and you're leaving?" However, before I could shift into disappointment mode…

"I know our relationship is young, but I would like for us to get married and for you and the kids to move with me to New York. I love all of you! I've always wanted children and I consider my meeting you as a blessing sent from God."

My mind races with thoughts bouncing from one side of my brain to the other.

"We have been together only two weeks and you want to get married? That is crazy!" I said. "And now, I am really considering it! That's even crazier!"

This is a big decision. I must consider my alternatives. I can stay here, continue working, continue raising my kids without a father, and continue to struggle. On the other hand, I can accept Paul's proposal of marriage. It seems like a no-brainer to me. I will gladly choose the latter!

We begin to make plans for the wedding and the move to New York. Jenny, the babysitter, suggests that we leave the kids in Texas while we take a honeymoon, moving our "stuff" to New York. We can go ahead and set up housekeeping. Later, I can return to pick up the kids.

"Jerome is the perfect baby and we really want to keep him as long as we can," they say. He actually knows her better than me, since she keeps him all day every day. Meanwhile, Mother decides she will keep Twan and Connie while Paul and I take our time moving north.

We ask Brenda and Phillip to stand with us at a small wedding in the Pastor's study.

Everything has been going like clockwork. On March 24, 1974 at the age of twenty-eight I marry Paul, age thirty-eight, in Longview, Texas.

A few days before renting a U-Haul trailer, I began discussing with Paul the things I should get rid of, since he had "better stuff."

"From my house, we will need beds for the kids and I want to take my kitchenware. YOUR big refrigerator will take up a lot of room."

"Oh, no!" he exclaims, "That's not mine! The furniture stays with the house. I'm renting everything!"

I swallow the lump in my throat, although I harbor it in my heart. I say nothing. We pack everything I have. After all, why should I be upset? My furniture is very nice and maybe I was wrong to assume that the nicer furniture BELONGED to him!

Now we are on our way to Newburgh, New York! I sold my car and we are driving Paul's Chevy pickup and pulling the largest U-Haul trailer available. It is fully loaded with all of my furniture, plus Paul's few personal belongings.

Why Bother?

I couldn't have planned it better
My desires just couldn't be met.
As my schedule wouldn't allow
What I wanted just wouldn't fit!

Planning and scheming
My desires to attain,
With these everyday pressures
My desires must remain.

No time for the foolishness
Of pleasure for me.
But, when left to God
He causes it to be!

Isn't it neat how God works for us!
Is not His love a gem?
God plans our days with vigilance and care,
If we only entrust them to Him!
　　　Suzie
Matt. 6:34, Prov. 27:1, James 4:13

Getting to Know Paul

Traveling together in the cab of Paul's pickup is actually the first time we have been alone. Paul and I are still getting to know one another. Within an hour of leaving east Texas, I suggest we play a little traveling game. I am thinking anybody can play this simple game.

"It's an **ABC** game! I look for something which starts with an **A**, like that airplane up there. That's my word, Airplane. Now, **B** is your letter and you find a **B** word."

"Baby," said Paul.

"Baby? Where do you see a baby? You have to see something that starts with "B".

"Oh! OK," he says nodding his head up and down. "But I'm sure there is a baby somewhere."

"Paul, pay attention to me.....*C* is the next letter. Look over there, see that cow? That's my word. C is for cow. Now it's your turn."

"I understand," Paul replies, ---- "Mailbox. There is a mailbox and we see it, right?"

"**D** is the next letter and it's your letter, but I'm just going to end this game right now with a **D** word, Dam!" I do NOT see a dam but I do feel the frustration. "Do you speak English? You say yes, but I don't think you *co-pre-hen-dee* at all!"

"Se señoría! Habla usted espanol?" he says.

The whole thing puts a bitter taste in my mouth and we are just getting started in our marriage. I silently begin to watch and notice things about Paul's behavior that I have never seen in anyone before. It never occurs to me that box starts with a *B*.

We have no problem finding a cute little house just outside the city of Newburgh. The location is close to Paul's job site and it looks to be a perfect place to start our life as a family.

To my surprise, Paul turns all of his personal business over to me. God has always blessed my finances so I certainly do not mind assuming the task of bookkeeping for our household. Upon examination of the budget, I realize Paul is in debt! He was living from paycheck to paycheck, and barely at that. Paul had indicated to me that he made a good salary and that there would be no problem with finances. In his personal records, I find he filed for bankruptcy two years ago!

I start to panic. What have I gotten us into? My plan to return to Texas to get the children and bring them back has me doubting! Throughout my marriage with Roy, we seldom lived above our means. We had no bills other than the monthly obligations of living, a house and car payments. I believe that accumulating debt is living above your means. I am very discouraged and think that maybe this "dream come true" could possibly become a "nightmare".

"Daddy, I think I've messed up! I made a mistake about Paul! There are a lot of things that aren't right. He has debt, he thinks differently than I do, and I don't think it's going to work." Over the phone, I muster the courage to admit it to Daddy and face my own mistake. I do not know what I expect Daddy to do or say. I am shocked as I listen to his response.

"Well, Suzie, you got married, you've moved all your belongings to New York, and everybody expects you back here next week to get the kids. You made your bed, so now I think you better just lie in it."

With that, I submit to his suggestion and decide to try to make the best of this situation. I put plane tickets on the credit card and fly to Texas. The next week the children and I are flying back to New York and our new home.

Paul is very happy. The kids rapidly take to him as he begins the role of father. Every weekend is filled with activities that range from driving into New York City, to going to Niagara Falls. We see and do everything the New England states have to offer!

I prayerfully and patiently take on the monthly budget, making double payments on credit cards. I scrimp, where possible, until the finances are finally in order. Bankruptcy indicates that budgeting had always been a problem with Paul. After a few months, I began controlling our finances instead of allowing our finances to control us!

Little things surface and I notice obvious irregularities in Paul's intellect. He has very little common sense. (After all, he married me!) He is persistent in the way he takes on a project and will eventually conquer any task at hand. *I will always admire him for that.*

Here is one example of a 'little thing'. I am an avid Dr. Pepper drinker. This has always been common knowledge to everyone who knows me. On our trip to New York, there were times when I made Paul go to several different gas stations so I could have a Dr. Pepper. I refused to drink anything else. In the 70's, Dr. Pepper was not readily available in all the states.

One day Paul comes home with a smile from ear to ear.

"Come with me and close your eyes," he said, taking my hand and leading me to his pickup. "Open wide to a big surprise!"

What did he have? Can you believe? He brought home, special for me, four six packs of Pepsi Cola.

I try to smile. The look behind that smile must have given it away. I have to tell him, "It's not Pepsi I love, it's Dr. Pepper." He was embarrassed and I felt sorry for him.

I bury feelings of disappointment and go with the flow! Paul is a good provider, a good father and yes, even a good husband. He gives one hundred percent of himself in every situation. I find that in my constant communication with God, I can be a good wife and with God's help, this family will survive.

> Continue to mumble and grumble
> Your life will surely take a tumble!
> With each new day I am learning,
> Only to God should I be turning.
> In a special way I am yearning,
> And anxiously waiting for His returning!
>   Suzie

"I am being transferred to Houston," said Paul. It has been less than a year.

"That's just a few hours from Winona. And, right next to Galveston!" I was excited to return to Texas.

We move to Channelview, a suburb of Houston. Mother's short visit to New York left the kids expressing their loneliness for friends, cousins and grandparents. In the back of my mind, I wonder if the Shamburgers will notice Paul's idiosyncrasies when they actually get to know him well. Even though my sister and I change our last name with each marriage, there is always the Shamburger factor.

The use of professional movers makes our move to Channelview a good one. We find a church we like and often make the trip to East Texas. Nobody ever mentions Paul's peculiarities although they are quite evident to me. His pleasant personality and his good heart give no cause for acquaintances to bring up the subject. Of course, he is my husband.

Roy stopped paying monthly child support as soon as Paul and I married. Paul is earning good money and supporting us well. He is a good father and there is no doubt that the kids love him as well. We approach Roy with a proposition:
"You will not owe any back child support if you will allow Paul to adopt the children and pay the legal fees for the adoption." Roy agrees, and Paul legally adopts the kids. At eighteen months old, Roy Jerome Eudy becomes Paul Jerome Murphy. The girls' last name, at five and seven, changes from Eudy to Murphy. Connie was in preschool and Twan was in first grade.

"What does it do?" I ask. "Is it like a toaster oven?"
"Watch!" said Paul. He puts in a half cup of water, closes the door with a click, turns a dial and the machine begins to hum with an electric sound. Thirty seconds later, there is a ding bell sound. "It's a microwave oven."
"Be careful!" I say, as Paul opens the door, reaches in and takes out half a cup of boiling water by the cup handle.
"See, it's not even hot!" Microwaves are just beginning to appear in retail stores. Paul surprises us by

bringing one home. We are among the first to acquire one.

"Wow, new technology is amazing! Who would have ever thought you could warm something up on a paper plate without catching the plate on fire. It is remarkable!"

Before the end of a year in Channelview, Paul's job sends us to Mobile, Alabama. We arrive at the beginning of a school term. Connie enters kindergarten and Twan is going into the third grade. Jerome is still at home. We are advised that the public schools are terrible, and we should enroll the kids in a private Christian school. There are many private schools to choose from and we select a small school, fairly close to our house. Later, I learn the reason for the creation of all the small private schools: integration and forced bussing!

We rent a house in a rural area of Mobile and buy the kids a pony. We spend most weekends sightseeing and hauling our bicycles to beautiful recreation spots, spending the day riding and picnicking. Twan rides her own bicycle, and mine has a seat on the back for hauling Connie. Paul rides his bicycle with Jerome in a child seat mounted on the back.

During the week, it is a bit lonely.

I am not pleased with the private school we picked. It has been a month and I feel the girls are not receiving a good education. It is more like home schooling, teaching in little groups. I investigate and find out the teachers are not certified.

About the time we are settling down in Alabama, Paul is transferred again. This time we travel to Canton, Ohio. The kids have only gone to school for a couple of months in Alabama and they will now finish out the year in the Ohio public school system. I welcome the move, not only because of the school situation, but also in Mobile, it seems impossible for me to hide my stress concerning Paul.

Ohio is a fun place to live. We start going to old estate sales and accumulate some very neat antiques! The highlight is exploring the old barns as well as the grounds of the old estate homes! The best sale we have gone to is at President McKinley's estate, where we bid and buy a nice collection of antiques.

I meet with neighbors and make new friends. I spend days attending bible study groups with several Christian women. Having activities outside the family is wonderful for my situation. My marriage is comfortable. This is confusing to me!

Perry and Marv come to Ohio for a visit. It is winter with lots of snow. We drive to New York City and have a wonderful time. Canton, Ohio is the home of the Pro Football Hall of Fame, so that is a must see!

During the summer, Mother flies to Canton and stays for a few weeks. The kids and I go back with her. We make the trip to Texas via locomotive! There is something majestic about riding and rocking, hearing and feeling the gentle clacking of the rails beneath you as you travel across this great country of ours. We have great time!

In almost every way, I have no complaints with life. The biggest thing missing is the emptiness I harbor in my heart.

After almost a year, it is back to Houston, a move which we did not see coming. However, we look forward to it. Texas feels like home and we will be much closer to my family.

We realize this move is not fair to the kids. They are in school and it is a problem, moving from place to place. Paul and I were blessed to spend our early years in stable environments.

We make a down payment on a house in Houston. The kids love their school and we quickly find a church we all like. Several families from the church become our friends. Although Paul has a long commute to and from work, he does not seem to mind.

Jerome is not yet in school and meets Jimmy, who lives two houses down. They are best friends! He has a little sister, Chantal, and they love staying and playing at our house. I begin caring for them while their parents work, making the grand sum of $50.00 a week. With my first paycheck, I immediately travel to a jewelry store in downtown Houston. They advertise diamonds for a very low price. Sure enough, I find the perfect, one carat, diamond for $600.00!

"Here is $50.00, for a lay-a-way down payment," I told the shopkeeper. Every week, for twelve weeks, I send my entire $50.00 paycheck. The jeweler mounts the diamond on a beautiful gold band and I am a happy lady. This $600.00 diamond is not just for show; it is an asset of good value, an investment.

"Perry Jo has been in an automobile accident!" It is a phone call from my brother, Mitchell.

"What happened?"

"A big seismograph truck pulled out in front of her little Porsche. She was on 155 and Sand Flat road at the city limit sign. I was not far behind. Suzie! She was holding her eyeball in her hand when I walked up to her crunched up car."

"So, how is she now?"

"She is in critical condition. She may lose an eye. She lost a kneecap; her jaw is broken and wired together. She is in intensive care and there may be brain damage."

I rush to Tyler and find her in the hospital in terrible condition. She is beyond recognition; her head is covered with bandages. She is in excruciating pain. Looking at my sister in such pain immediately broke my heart. I wished that I could somehow take the pain for her. If it were possible, I would gladly trade places with her. This is my first experience as an intercessor.

Paul takes off work to take care of the kids so I can stay with Perry for several days. I feel useless knowing there is nothing I can physically do to help. We pray fervent prayers.

"Do you want a valium?" Donna asks. She is one of the weekly card players that goes to Perry's on weekends.

"No. I'm ok," I answer.

"I don't know how your whole family can be so calm. I'm climbing the walls and you guys are holding it together so well."

"It is a matter of faith. Even if God chooses to take her right now, we know that life is not over with the last breath we take. We have confidence that whatever the outcome, things will be OK. God is in control."

"I feel your pain," I said to Perry.

"You don't know what pain is," she said. "Unless you have been there you can't know how it feels."

The doctors do a wonderful job putting Perry Jo back together. Everything, even her eye, seems to work.

I reluctantly return to Houston wishing I could do

more to help my sister in the long slow process of healing.

REST

As we seek to help others,
As we seek to do God's will;
'Tis hard to rest in Jesus
Just to wait and to be still.

Over anxious and in a hurry,
Wanting to conquer trials quick,
'Tis hard to accept God's timing,
It is He who makes time click!

God is in control of time,
Master of all for sure.
He wants us to pause and relax,
Allowing Him to solve and cure.

God can do it, yes He does.
Why underestimate His power?
God's love indeed abounds for us
He controls with each passing hour.
        Suzie

Chapter 8
New Awakening

In Houston, I experienced a new awakening! As a Christian, I have studied God's Word continually. Yet I had never actually examined the many aspects of God's Spirit!

"Dust to dust, ashes to ashes. We lay this body in the grave, but the spirit is going to be with the Lord," How many times have I heard that at funerals and in sermons? I began to think about my spirit.

"You must be born again," said Jesus. (Born of the Spirit). That is what I had read and what I was taught. When the Holy Spirit takes abode in us, it somehow attaches to our spirit, thus our old spirit has become new! Through Christ, the Holy Spirit and our spirit have become one. My spirit becomes our Spirit.

The apostle, Paul, was speaking to us when he wrote; "To be absent from the body is to be present with The Lord!" Second Corinthians 5:5-9. (NIV) This scripture was only words on a page. I knew intellectually, yet I had not experienced it. I can liken it unto the Holy Spirit in the Old Testament. He appeared and disappeared at will. When I needed The Spirit, He was there. Otherwise, The Spirit remained dormant. I was not conscious of The Spirit's continual presence in my life. At that time, if my spirit were to leave my body, more than likely, I would not even know it. I have always known I had the Spirit. I never actually considered it a real thing, something of weight and size. Should I be fully aware of my spirit at all times?

I developed a hunger to learn about the Spirit. What

better place to go than to the Book written by the Spirit? I enveloped myself in God's Word. "In the beginning was the Word..." My hunger would not allow me to put the Bible down. For weeks, as soon as the kids left for school, I began reading and I was still reading when they returned home. I did not want to stop reading! I marveled at words I had read so many times before. This time the veil was lifted and new understanding was apparent. The words supernaturally came alive. "Sharper than any double-edged sword, it penetrates even to dividing soul and spirit, joints and marrow; it judges the thoughts and attitudes of the heart." (Hebrews 4:12) For the first time in my life, the words came alive! I fed my Spirit and the Word became a part of me.

Since that realization, I have witnessed the acts of the Spirit living in me. I have been conscious of the Spirit helping me pray. I have even been aware of times when the Spirit within me ached with sadness. Still, I did not realize the Spirit was actually part of me.

A whole new world seemed to emerge! I experienced a new dimension. As I read the words of the apostles, I became aware that they not only knew the Spirit lived within them, but they were continually living through and drawing strength from the Spirit. Most impressive of all, they listened and allowed the Spirit to direct their every step. Wow! That was a study where God revealed himself in a mighty way. It was an astounding experience which changed my life.

I know very well the Spirit which lives in me. I now know that when I die, my Spirit will go to be with the Lord. I will be fully aware of the goings on. I try to obey the Spirit's direction, yet I often fall short. There is a battle within me, a battle that confronts all Christians. There is a constant uprising between the Spirit and the flesh: good and evil.

If I had NOT gone to God's Word for answers,   I would still be ignorant of Living in the Spirit.

REVELATION

Searching scripture for answers,
Desiring to be fed,
Turning to God's word,
Adsorbing what it says.

Words spring from the page,
The exact answer we need,
God knows when we're hungry,
Our appetite He feeds.

Opening the eyes of our heart,
Confirmation and scriptures unfold,
New Light in meaning comes to us,
As God's performance, we behold!

Suzie

The Accident
Part 3
Words from Others

A small spiral notebook appeared in Elizabeth's hospital room on her first day in Midland. When it was full another one appeared. Here are a few entries.

2-17-08 Elizabeth - Here you are, lying in the hospital tubes coming out from everywhere. Not fun for you or any of us. (Your family) We can tell you are frustrated, and we are frustrated because we can't fix your problems.

My prayers are for your full recovery and I know there are many others praying the same.

Cindy is very unhappy out in Arizona, as are Morgan and Mimi and others. In Texas, I can't begin to name, names, but today is Sunday and I know God has heard from many voices. I have had the experience of burying two husbands and a child and I fully believe God will NOT allow me the experience of losing my sister. So I am full of hope and faith for your getting well. Love you and hope that after you get well, you will enjoy our little notes of love. Love! Perry

2-17-08 4 pm - - MOM, We're here and just picked up your things from the van. It's a big mess and we see how you must have gotten hurt. Now you're trying to write messages - and taking control. But you need to just REST! I can see how strong you are and although I already knew, I'm still impressed. On our travel here (Twan and I flew) people just noticed we are the type who are happy or well spirited.....We told them we got it from our Mother and we are going to Midland for a sad scary reason.......What our Mother instilled in us is so deep - it will always shine through! You are a wonderful woman - a loved woman - a cherished woman - and a loved Mother!

After this, though, we're going to be making some new rules ====Connie

Feb 17, 2008 - - Mom,
Some people say that you don't know what you've got until it's gone.
Well that's NOT the case with how I feel about you. I love you every day and I cherish you for all the joy and goodness that you bring into my life. I don't ever want to spend a long amount of time without talking to you. I cherish every phone call – every silly conversation – and the things that we laugh at that most people don't find funny!
I have always known that you are the best mother that I could have! It doesn't take a tragedy for me to realize how special you are or how much I love you. But it did make me realize that I am a pathetic mess of emotion – I love you – I am happy that you are feeling better. I hope you can talk before I have to leave to go home. Just don't slap me like you did Jerome. ☺ Twan

My Favorite Aunt – Hey Aunt Elizabeth – You are so stubborn and we are all sorry we can't understand your lip smacking or air painting with your finger! We love you so much! We are just as frustrated as you are! We are so happy you're alive! Get well Soon! XoxoxO Love always – Marlee

5:40 pm - - Elizabeth, I can't believe this is happening to you. Now it seems everything will be all right. I have realized really how blessed this family is. No one is taken for granted. At any moment if God took away anyone of your family members there would be no doubt to that person how much they are loved and would be missed. I am praying for you and Ron and so is all my family and friends. We love you beyond words! Love Michelle (daughter in law)

7:30 am 2-18-08   Good morning Mom!   You're beautiful......☺ It was nice to see your bright eyes. Even the nurses say you have beautiful eyes.

I didn't stay last night, because I feel like you'll make me break the rules. You just tried to get me to help you get out of bed! NOPE – Can't do it......SILLY ☺ ... Anyways now you're trying without me. It is president's day and I wish I could just stay until you go home!

You just flipped and they said they are trying to remove that breathing tube today. Your respiratory therapist, Evelyn and today's nurse are careless.

You look sort of comfy (smile) I mean except for the hoses – cords – incision – broken hand – bruises- that type of stuff. ☹

This kind of thing is a real reminder of how sweet this gift of life is (from God) and how fragile it is.

Our bodies and how they work-function and even come back after such traumas, AMAZING.

I like to see how you resting. Right now I just wanted to come to your side and chat. Talk about something silly . . . Hear you laugh – see your smile. But I guess we'll do that later. Right?

That bridge was covered in ICE ... There were 20 wrecks from Friday night (10 pm) 2/16/08 thru Sat. night 2/17/08. Just so many cars on that icy bridge. . . Dangerous, we're lucky you're here and that Ron is OK.

Did I tell you – the nurses get annoyed with us – because we all want to be here – and they say we over stimulate you. Ha Ha --- LOL Twan

So far the people here are: Jerome & Michelle (Evie & Jacob), Connie, Twan, Aunt Perry, Marlee, Ron (of course) Today's expected arrivals: Lolo, Uncle Mitch & Aunt Faye, Jeann Gardner. So many people want to be by your side. You are always there for everybody else and it's like we want to return that feeling. I'm running out for a few - but will be back. I love you Mom. Connie

Monday Feb. 18   11:42 am Nurses today are being mean to us. The nurses yesterday were nicer. You look better today but you are irritated with me for some reason. I think I will have to go home tomorrow. LoLo and Mitch will be here today. Dalys called and wants me to let you know that she loves you very much and she is praying for you. Love, Twan

Mom, just wanted to let you know how much I love you!! You have given us (Connie, Twan & I) the best life and I am so proud that you are my mother. At first, it was very scary to think of losing you, but now things look really good and I just can't wait for you to get out of the hospital. I love you! So does Jacob & Evie. Evie is getting mad because she really wants to see Grandma Cole!! Jerome

Mom – When I got here at the hospital the day of the accident you were completely sedated and it made me cry a lot. I slept in the room in a chair and watched the monitors. Your heart rate was 101. Your blood pressure was 70 and you were on a breathing machine 100%. Today is day #3 and your heart rate is 88, your blood pressure is 123 and they just turned off the respirator and you are breathing 100% on your own. You are getting better! Yay! Twan

Prayers are with you! Joliette Harris
God bless and protect you. May you heal quickly. Cathy Carruth, Midland friends of Carolyn Curtis from Winona.

2-18-08 6 pm Well things are settling down in your room. Me, and Mom, are getting a good visit. You seem to be much more comfortable on your side (Who wouldn't be?)Your ears are the only holes that don't have a tube in it and I know they are uncomfortable. I'm sure the remainder of this occasion will be like remembering a root canal. Anyway – lots of prayers from Billy Price and friends you don't even know to our family, all of us who care for you very much. I think your improvement will be faster than expected. Unfortunately, as you get better aches and pain will get worse. Get well, Love Mitch Yo little Brother

Today is a joy. Just to see you and know that God spared you for more good works. You are the best. It grieves me that I didn't kiss you good-bye the night before you left. I was so tired from "Dallas" that I just went to sleep. I treasure your note. You are so improved compared – Thank God! He is so good to us. I am sure you will look back at this one-day and think of it as a bad dream.   I was a basket case until I got here and saw you for myself. You are my precious baby I love you, Lolo Mother

Things are looking up! It appears the surgery was a success, Elizabeth's vitals are getting stronger and the only thing left to do is begin the long road to recovery! Praise The Lord for answered prayer! The continuation of this journey will be a long tedious one. Especially for Elizabeth. Flora, Your Nurse for the night.

Again to MY favorites Aunt! I love you and am sorry you wrecked! You are doing so wonderful! I'm so happy you're getting better! I love you so much! God has blessed you and all of us! All my Love Marlee Dean

Mom, Twan and I head out tomorrow. I'm so sad and wish I could be here until you get out. You take it easy; listen to the doctors and nurses! I can't wait to see you again! I know you'll feel better then. I love you, Mom. Connie

Mom, Goodnight it's 9:20 pm on Monday – I have to leave tomorrow early...I guess I will see you in a few weeks. I love you very much – and I will be calling you soon. I love you Mom. Twan

Elizabeth,
Roses are red
Violets are blue
 Got out of bed
Shame on you! ☺

Your progress is miraculous – I am so happy. I just pray your good health will keep returning. Maybe even with the new blood you'll be healthier. Love! Your Sister Perry 2/20/08

Everyone is encouraged and is seeing improvement! You are talking and joining in on conversations, as much as possible. I know it is difficult with that huge tube going down your throat,

My dear Elizabeth, When I got the call telling me that you were in an accident, my heart stopped because I can't imagine my world without you in it. You are my strength when I'm down and you are the person I want to share my joys with. True friends we have been now for 10 odd years and many adventures we've shared. I pray that God will give us many more opportunities. Your BFF, Jeann

2/21/08 Elizabeth, You had your first liquid food today. More tubes out!
2/22/08 Good night – taking Maalox, etc. For gas. Lots of pretty flowers and cards! Love Perry
2/23/08 My vacation in Midland, Texas by Perry.
Early morning, no sun, cigarette and coffee, I'm sitting out at the entrance of the hospital. Beautiful pines full of cooing doves – getting their day started. All is quiet except the cooing. How peaceful is Midland!

Elizabeth report: Things she can do: 1. Burp, 2. Sit up, 3. Brush teeth, 4. Comb hair, 5. Begin to show signs of ethnic blood. Behavior slightly modified (ha!), 6. Wants to wash hair.

2/24/08 The hospital runs a skeleton crew on Sundays. Lolo is at the motel, not sick, but in the bed. Elizabeth is up and down. All tubes but oxygen removed!

2/25/08 Physical therapist walked Elizabeth 25 feet on a walker. Colon attacked by bacteria. The cause is from original antibiotics. New antibiotics administered to kill the bacteria.

2/26/08 Bacteria causes very foul diarrhea. Unable to control - - Slow to get cleaned up, very depressing. No more morphine. Hydrocodone 500mg. 2 pills.

2/27/08 Can't use hydrocodone. Messes with gas pains. Maalox. Elizabeth still has diarrhea, hopefully some control tomorrow evening. Gas & pain. ☹

Elizabeth has improved sooooooo much. :-) Now she is aware of how miserable she really is. She requires 2 nurses at a time. Me and Perry! We are glad we are here to run around the bed waiting on her. She does want a lot. ☹ God Bless. It will be bad to see her go west and for me to go east. Thank God, I am able to stay here and be a part of her healing. After all, she is a product of me. Love her, Lolo

2/28/08 Well here it is Thursday. Hopefully this is the day before the big trip to Arizona. The diarrhea is cut in half. Going $\frac{1}{2}$ the times in these 12 hours as the last 12 hours. Still cannot get into bed by herself. Can get up on the walker out of bed.

Elizabeth, I will miss getting up before dawn and running in to see how your night went and how your day is beginning. I hope with rehab that you will quickly regain your strength and be up and going soon. If you feel they are tough on you, they are there to rehabilitate you and know your limits. Sometimes you are capable of more than you know. The best to you! Love Perry

One more day! Much progress has been made. You called the motel at 6:00 am asking for cheese and crackers. You ate bowl of grits with 4 tsp. of sugar, and drank orange juice. Nurse removed central line from neck. Home today?
"If you will please get well, I will take you on a vacation to HAWAII!" Brad

Life goes on. Even though time seems to have stopped when we heard the news, it is now time to continue on life's journey. Michelle with Evie (3) and Jacob (8) must return to Arizona. We rented a motel room in Midland during our stay and it is time for us to go. Looks like you are going to be OK. See you soon. Jerome

Honey, I have never seen so many cards and flowers in one room! And you say you don't even know some of these people! It is amazing but we are going to have to clear out some of it. Bettie from Housekeeping

From Ron,
I am so sorry this happened. I am still hurting from head to toe. I'm sore and bruised all over. There is nothing else I can do here. You have plenty of company and you sister is here all the time. The rest of the Texas group is ready to caravan east.
I miss Cleo so much and we think Buffy will be better off in East Texas until I can get around better.
Jeann has returned to her home in D.C. and Twan and Connie went to the airport for their return flight to California.
Although Jerome and Michelle live one hundred fifty miles short of Scottsdale, they have offered to drive me home. I dread the long ride to Arizona.

Lolo and Perry are staying here and they say you will be able to go to Scottsdale in a few days.

Bye for now. Come home soon.

Love,

Ron

And, there are cards and letters. "Get Well" cards, "Miss You" cards, "Hang in There" cards, "The Bible Says" cards, and "Funny" cards."

"What is this?" Lolo ask looking at the picture of a skinny brown cow chewing on a clump of straw. "It is a card from Gary John Wyman!"

"It looks like my old high school flame finally cares," says Elizabeth. A hilarious card arrives each week from him. They are totally country and can make even the sickest person laugh. Elizabeth laughs as she reads the card.

"That's a miracle, laughing in the shape you're in," says Lolo.

All the cards and letters are read and appreciated. Elizabeth cannot write back. All she can do is try to write on the marking board with a broken wrist!

One card has money and a note, "Someone said you wanted a hamburger so here is a five dollar bill. Tell them to get you a hamburger!" Love You, Helen Bozeman.

This is our last night in Midland! Our hearts are somber and we are weary. It has been a long battle and we all survived this ordeal. Tomorrow you will be on your way to Arizona, where you will heal! Love, Perry

I know you came back to the apartment to retrieve the special cross you designed many years ago. You were wearing it at the time of the accident. I will wear and care for it until I give it back to a well and healthy Daughter! Love Always Lolo.

PS. The Waterford vase I will care for also!

After a good night's sleep, Lolo and Perry return to the hospital and thank Dr. Sawyer and the medical team for their dedication and for helping our family.

Elizabeth still can do very little for herself. Her dependence on Leola and Perry causes her to dread leaving the hospital.

Elizabeth looks out the back windows of the ambulance to see Lolo and Perry peering in. They are excited to see her well enough to travel. Elizabeth feels all alone.

Passing through Colorado City, Lolo and Perry take time to find the ambulance service that saved Elizabeth's life. They personally thank the emergency crew who cared for Ron and Elizabeth.

"We are excited to see you! We get very involved with patients during the actual occurrence, but we very seldom learn the outcome. Rarely does anyone return to say thank you."

As far as they all know, Elizabeth will arrive safely at her next hospital destination in Arizona. Little did they know the pain she was experiencing! What is more, little did Elizabeth know this would be a trip straight through the pits of hell!

Chapter 9
Preparation for Saudi Arabia

All is well and life is running smoothly. The family is happy and I appear to be happy. I manage to suppress my inner feelings.

"I have an opportunity with a new company called HBH," Paul announces. "The pay is unbelievable. We would make enough money to live well and have a good nest egg when we come back. They have a contract to build a Navy Base in Saudi Arabia."

"How long?" I ask.

"It's a four year contract, but we get a month of paid vacation for every six months we live in Saudi! This is a new experience for the Saudi government and HBH. We are the guinea pigs."

"Of course, take it!" I respond. "The benefits are great and it sounds very exciting to all of us!" The Spirit within me jumps for joy!

We immediately prepare for our new adventure. Within two weeks, the house is sold. The school year is over so school is not a problem. We apply for passports.

Movers come, pack all of our personal belongings, and move it all to storage in Tyler.

"This is going to cost a fortune," I grumble.

"There are no out of pocket expenses. HBH pays for moving, storage and everything; even our meals, until we get to our destination," Paul answers. We plan to stay in Winona with Mother and Daddy for a few days.

Paul goes to Washington D.C. for briefings, while we wait for our passports. We will join him in Washington, once the passports arrive and then we will all leave for Saudi, together.

The day comes when we are going to Washington

fully expecting to fly out.

"Sorry, there is a problem with the Visas. Mr. Murphy's work Visa is ready," the HBH clerk holds up the open passport. "See, it is stamped, so he's good to go." He goes without us. The kids and I go back to my parent's home in Winona while we wait for our Visas to clear.

"We are not sure what the problem is." Says the Bureau of Consular Affairs, which is part of the US Department of State. "Or if there is a problem. We will notify you when your Visas are ready."

"They were supposed to be ready for us two weeks ago," I exclaimed.

"There are certain restrictions of travel to some countries. I will forward your concern."

This does not sound very promising and I do not want to wear out my welcome with Mother and Daddy. God provides a perfect answer. Six miles from Winona, is Owentown, where a small group of new homes are for sale, with an $850.00 down payment.

"The diamond ring is valued at $1,400.00," the jeweler says.

"I'll take it!"

"Well it doesn't quite work like that. I will give you $850."

I buy one of the houses for us to stay in until we can leave. I see this as another good investment.

Staying in the unfurnished house is much like camping out. Friends let us borrow a few necessities to get by. Days turn into weeks. Paul is in Saudi Arabia, and HBH keeps us apprised of the status of our departure date.

After two months, the time arrives. We receive airline tickets to return to Washington D.C. Paul is returning from Saudi to escort us to the Middle East.

We are ecstatic! I rent out the house and realize it is a good investment.

With five oversized suitcases, we are finally leaving for Saudi! We fly into D.C. where Paul is waiting at the airport with a rental car.

"Did you pack the kitchen sink?" Paul asks looking at the huge pile of luggage. "We have to hire a taxi just to transport the luggage."

Washington D.C. is exciting! Our passports are not stamped so we cannot leave the United States.

Paul calls the office each morning.

"The passports are not stamped." For us that means another glorious day of sightseeing!

Washington D.C. is definitely a city every American should visit. So much government! Each and every building is an impressive monument in itself.

"If you think about it," I say looking around, "since this is all government, in a small twisted way, it belongs to us!" We sightsee and ponder the magnificence of everything!

We go to the Smithsonian Institution for several days. The Smithsonian is a group of museums that would take weeks to go through. We go outside the city to Georgetown; we see the Arlington National Cemetery. We also spend a day exploring the Potomac River.

"This week has been such a blessing!" I tell Paul. "What the devil intended for bad, God exchanged it for our good." The disappointment of not leaving for Saudi on time is erased by the great adventures we are having.

"The block of family Visas is a Saudi problem. And Allah (God) only knows when you will be able to travel," says the man with HBH. "It's been over a week and, Paul, we need you back in Saudi. Now! We'll let you know more when we find out more. The wife and kids can stay in Washington or go back to Missouri."

"It's Texas."

"Oh, sorry. Texas. Stay or go, it is all on the HBH expense account."

"We have a lot of baggage here."

"No problem. Leave it at the hotel. We have a running contract with them." The man sounds like he has been through this before.

"Mother," I say sheepishly on the phone. "We are on our way back." I am embarrassed.

Not knowing how much longer it will be before we try to leave again, I take the opportunity to buy another house! This time it was nothing down and closing costs were very little. We borrow the same sheets, towels, and mattresses as before and a few pots and pans. We are camping indoors again, until further notice.

"Yes, we are still here." I have to explain to my friends and family. They, in their own way, are impatiently waiting; just as we are for our journey to begin. It is awkward trying to keep friends up to date and exclaiming again and again, "We're still here."

Fall arrives and it is time to enroll the kids in school, or not! This is a new protocol for HBH; they have no way of giving me a time period. I made a wise decision and enrolled the kids in the Winona school. They have been in school for almost a whole semester and it happens! We receive news that the family can definitely join Paul in a few days.

"Hello, is this Suzie?" The voice on the phone is slow and strangely familiar.

"May I ask who is calling?"

"It's Roy, I mean I am Roy," he talks a little slurred. "Are you happy?"

"Well, I guess I am as happy as I can be."

"I think leaving you might have been a mistake," says Roy.

"Mistake or not it is water under the bridge now. Have you been drinking?"

"Why don't we get back together? I'll dump Georgia and you can divorce what's-his-name and we can start all over or pick up where we were."

I think about it for about two seconds, "It has been seven years Roy. I have survived on my own, thank you. I am on my way to Saudi Arabia and I am going to see the world. I wish you the best but us getting back together is something that will not happen!"

To my amazement, Pete and Donna Roberts have a lovely going away party in my honor! How nice! There are many people wishing me von-voyage! Some give gag gifts like the one from Victor and Lorene Kay. It is a round wooden coin with the words "TO-IT" written on one side! The card attached says, "We're glad you finally got a ROUND-TO-IT."

Now I am a landlord with three houses!

After eleven months of waiting, planning and almost leaving several times, we meet Paul in Washington, D.C. and are finally on a plane toward Saudi. It is June 30, 1980, I am thirty-five years old, Twan is almost fourteen, Connie is nearing ten and Jerome is seven.

Our complicated and delayed departure is not a unique story. I learn that it happens to most families and seems to be a pre-requisite for going to Saudi. The

Arabian government is reluctant to give Visas to family members of workers. Work Visas are hard to obtain and there is no such thing as a tourist Visa. The Saudis are a very private country.

Our first stop is a three-day layover in Paris, France. This is our first international trip as a family. We disembark the plane for a very fast and drizzling, wet tour of Paris. This is also our first experience of clearing immigrations and customs. We learn the international airport hoop-la. It is a chore everyone wishes to avoid, but there is no way out.

In Paris, the beautiful buildings and other sights dazzle us. Twan has a terrible case of jet lag.

"Just leave me alone," she complained. "I have a headache and I just want to be left alone in the hotel room."

"No way," I protest. "Chances like this come once in a lifetime and you are not going to say you spent three days in a hotel room in Paris."

Drug her all over Paris and she disappeared at the Eiffel Tower.

"What are you doing?" I ask. Twan steps back to reveal her name scribbled on the Eiffel Tower.

We loved the pastry shops and bought the long loaves of bread. Although there were sidewalk cafes everywhere, we sat on the sidewalk and had our own little picnic.

The children and I cram into a public bus with what seems like a thousand people.

As the bus starts to roll, I look through the frosted window.

"Paul," I screech, as I watch him fade away still

standing on the corner! We have no choice but to continue our sightseeing without him. He is waiting when we return to the hotel.

"A thousand dollars!" When we check out of Paris with our eight suitcases, we are charged an extra thousand dollars for the excess baggage. I am shocked, but HBH pays it without blinking an eye.

From Paris our flight was direct to Saudi Arabia.

True Blessing

God has so blessed
I'll try to convey
How mightily
God is performing today!

God has so blessed
In truth word and deed
In every circumstance
Filling each need!

God has so blessed.
Gray skies He transforms.
Protecting us daily
Through every storm!

God has so blessed
Achieving His goal
Bless the Lord
Oh My Soul!
  Suzie

True blessing comes not in material matter.
It isn't wealth laid out on a platter.
True blessings are gifts for the inner being.
I pray you understand what I am seeing.

If these words to you sound odd,
Please examine your relationship with God.
Words in Romans contain this thought.
They also say, by His blood we were bought.

Suzie

Read Romans 8:28-34
Praise the Lord for True Blessing!

(In part from *Wikipedia*)
Saudi Arabia is in the Middle East.

The history of Saudi Arabia, as a state, began with King Abdulaziz Al Saud. The human history of the region extends as far back as 20,000 years ago. The region has had a global impact twice in world history. The first was in the 7th century when it became the cradle of Islam. The second was in the mid-20th century with the discovery of vast oil deposits. The cities of Mecca and Medina have the highest spiritual significance for the Muslim world. Mecca is the destination for the Hajj annual pilgrimage.

The Al Saud leader, Abdulaziz, carried out a series of wars resulting in the creation of the Kingdom of Saudi Arabia in 1932.

Since 1932, Saudi Arabia has been an absolute monarchy. King Faisal presided over a period of growth and modernization fueled by oil wealth. Saudi Arabia's role in the 1973 oil crisis, and, the subsequent rise in the price of oil, dramatically increased the country's political significance and wealth. The reign of his successor, Khalid, saw the first major signs of dissent with the seizure of the Grand Mosque in Mecca by Islamist extremists in 1979. Fahd became king in 1982 and, during his reign, Saudi Arabia became the largest oil producer in the world.

Chapter 10
In and Out of Saudi

We step off the plane in Saudi Arabia and stand by the aircraft door. From the top of the mobile steps we view our new homeland. Seven-year-old Jerome is holding my hand.

"Mom, it's HOT!" The heat blasts us in the face and it feels as though we have stepped into an oven. Texas summers can be mighty hot, but I have never felt heat like this. It is 118 degrees!

We line up with other passengers going through passport control. We gather up our eight huge suitcases and all our carry-on luggage and head to customs. Three hours later, we proceed outside into darkness where an HBH van is waiting.

"It is going not all to fit," alleges our foreign driver, with a strange accent. He is a little man with dark skin. "We wait for another van for luggage."

It is one o'clock in the morning when we walk into the front door. "The house is huge and very nice. We are so excited!" I say, approvingly, to Paul.

"I'm so glad you are finally ALL here," he replies, with a big grin on his face.

We are wide-awake and the kids are exploring the four bedrooms, two large living areas, two big bathrooms, a game room, and a tremendous dining area. The kitchen is equipped with everything a person could dream of and everything in the house is new. The furniture is beautiful. This house is like a dream come true!

On the coffee table is a cake and a card saying, "Welcome to Saudi."

Ding-dong goes the doorbell and we have visitors at

this hour!

"We are the Muñozes, and we have been waiting for you!" A line of kids come in and introduce themselves to our kids. We finally go to bed before the sun comes up.

The next few days are a blur. Jet lag lands right on my head…There seems to be a continuous line of ladies coming in and out, in and out, in and out!

"Are they being friendly, or, are they checking me out?" I ask. I do not know which.

"We have heard so much about you from Paul, we are expecting great things from your family!" This seems to be a common theme coming from the visitors. I believe Paul has stirred up the curiosity.

As jet lag fades, we have no problem settling in. We all like Saudi very much. Paul paved the way for our entry by telling everyone how wonderful we are! Paul has proven himself a gossip in the past and I can tell immediately that living in this small community will give him the opportunity to buzz like a bee! Gossiping is bad enough, but Paul's biggest problem is, he gets over half of the information wrong.

Paul has two beautiful blond dogs that look a lot like gray hounds. They are Arabian Sulkies. The rest of us do not really want them, but he does. He loves to walk them daily around the base. I figure doing so gives him a chance to speak to everyone and learn the latest scoop so he will be on top of everything.

We live in the city of Jubial in a specific area called "The Base." One day it will be a Saudi Arabian Navy Base. They have no navy so the US Government graciously consented to contract a company to build a base for them. This contract is on the Saudi's dime. Once the buildings are constructed, we will send our Navy to train their men. Three companies joined together. (**Hughes**

Aircraft Co., **B**endix Corp. and **H**olmes & Narver Inc.)
The company **HBH** was created for this project.

"Mama! Come look in the back yard!" exclaims
Jerome. "There's a turtle!"

I am thinking of the turtles we dodge crossing the
highways in East Texas. This turtle would total any car
that hit it. It is a huge sand turtle. When I say huge, I am
talking about a turtle whose shell is at least three feet
across his back!

"Let's call him Sylvia!" says Twan, straddling him
like a horse. The turtle does not move except to lift a giant
head and look around with black dime-size eyes.

Sylvia is very slow, eats dog food, and drinks the
water we leave out for him or her. One day Sylvia
disappears. We know not where.

Want to learn a sport? There are free tennis lessons,
swimming lessons, pool lessons, sailing lessons, square
dancing, name almost anything and it is available for
adults and children. We actually lack for nothing.

Filipinos are wonderful workers in Saudi and part of
their job is to entertain the American families. They are
such a likeable group of men. In their time off, they
become "houseboys" for the ladies and keep the houses
beautifully clean.

October 1980

"We are going back to the USA," I announce.
"With stopovers in Rome and Greece!"

We have been here for four months and it is time for
R&R (Rest and Relaxation).

It is raining in Rome, but not enough to keep us from seeing every sight. We spend one morning chasing cats all over the Roman Coliseum. It is lovely romping and playing on stadium benches built over 1900 years ago. Over 200 stray cats are scampering around. A few are friendly, most are not.

On the bus ride to Vatican City, the guide warns everyone, "Watch your belongings. The pickpockets! They are always waiting just outside the Vatican walls. They are looking for tourists and anyone who has something of value. If they touch you, like magic, your billfold, purse, watch, money, whatever they want is gone!"

Since we were warned, I feel sure we will have no problem.

After a tour inside the Vatican, we are given free time to explore. As we walk outside, a small group of people seems to pass through and among us. I notice a woman quickly brush against Paul. We push our way through the group.

"They didn't get your wallet did they?" I comment to Paul.

"No way, I took it out of my back pocket and put it right here," he says, tapping his right hand over his left shirt pocket. "I have it right here, here, here..." As he is speaks he realizes his wallet is gone! Quickly he whips around and points to the woman and shouts, "She took my wallet! My wallet is gone!"

A guard happens to be standing close by and stops the woman.

The conversation is in Italian, but I can tell she is adamantly saying "No not me!" and "He is mistaken."

I am almost convinced it was not her, when the guard shakes her long skirt and out falls the wallet!

"Thank you so much," Paul responds while taking

the wallet. "You are a lifesaver."

The guard smiles and tips his head as though it is just another day at work. We quickly go straight to the bus where we find two other victims who did not get their wallets back.

We leave Italy three days earlier than planned. Maybe we are a little homesick for the United States.

We are all very happy to be back in the USA. Four months seems longer when you are on the other side of the earth. The Middle Eastern culture has rubbed off on us and it takes a day or two to get back into the swing of normalcy. The children are anxious to see their old friends, and tell them about their new lives. I have fun showing photos to friends and family and enjoy answering questions.

Well, it is fun for two weeks. Now we are all anxious to get back to our new "home" in the Middle East, or at least, get back on the road again, or in the air!

"Next stop is Greece where we will spend a week," I tell the kids.

We land in Athens where it is cool and comfortable. We tour the city in scattered rain showers.

I especially love the two-day tour of Corinth. For me, Corinth is spectacular. The apostle Paul was in Corinth when he wrote the Epistles to several of the early churches.

We visit a boarding school, TASIS/Hellenic International School, where several of Twan and Connie's friends go. I want to expose Twan to the school to see if she would like to go. We have a great time dining with their friends.

"Do you think boarding school is something you

would like?" I ask Twan.

"Mom, I have no desire to go there, now or ever!"

We do a lot of walking in Greece and see all of the sights including the Acropolis with its beautiful Parthenon. It is truly magnificent.

Saudi is all we remembered it to be! The daily routine is   tennis, aerobics, women group outings, swimming and coffees. The kids go to a private school in Bechtel, another community about fifteen miles from ours. They return each day with enthusiasm.

I become a school bus monitor going to Bechtel School every morning and afternoon. This takes a chunk out of my day and forces me to get up early. The pay is $50.00 an hour for 3 hours a day – TAX FREE! It is fun with all the kids on the bus.

"You're fired," Paul informs me. "The Saudis have discovered that women are working. That is a no-no here."

"You mean I have been doing this for five months and now I can't do it anymore?"

"Welcome to Saudi Arabia. From now on the school buses will be monitored by Filipinos."

We find some special friends in Saudi. Richard and Nita Brighton are older than we are with no children accompanying them. Nita takes to Twan, Connie and Jerome immediately and we become good friends.

Christmas time approaches. All of us are far away from moms, dads, Yuletide friends, and families.

"What can we do to make it feel like Christmas around here?" Nita ask. "What do you miss the most?"

"Christmas Dinner!" is my answer. The elaborate, sit down, Christmas Dinner plans start with us and grows to include other people and later other families.

"We can use one of the nice multi-purpose rooms," says Nita.

"That kind of defeats the purpose of an intimate atmosphere." I pause. "Since my house is one of the largest ones on base, let's have it here."

We have a sit down dinner for 130 people! Several other women help, but Nita and I do most of the work. We have tables and chairs brought in and hire Filipinos to serve and clean up. We share gifts and "Ho ho ho!" Santa Claus even shows up. Everyone loves it. What a wonderful Christmas!

In January, Paul and Dennis have a business meeting in London, England. Dennis's wife, Lynda, and I take this opportunity to join them. We pled our case and the trip extends with two more weeks of adventure!

Nita insist on keeping the kids! I completely trust her and I know she will enjoy the task. Besides, I figure, Paul will return in only a few days to take over their care.

Lynda and I meet our husbands in London and stay with them for four days. While they work during the day, we go sightseeing. In the evenings, we all dine out and do fun things like the "Evening Lights" tour. London is beautiful at night. We take in the play "Annie." London is better than we had imagined.

The men are going to leave London on Friday so on Thursday Linda and I fly to Amsterdam to spend three days. It is cool in Europe, but the chill does not keep us from museums and galleries. We see "Night Watch" by Rembrandt and there is a huge display of Van Gogh's paintings. One tour of Amsterdam includes Anne Frank's house!

From Holland, we fly to Frankfort, Germany, and take a train to Baumholder, where I lived with Roy in the Army. Twan was born in Neubrooke, just outside of Baumholder. We go to the house where we lived and talk with our old German landlord and his family. They are happy to visit and reminisce. They even take us to a guesthouse (German Restaurant) for dinner.

Germany is very cold with a lot of snow. We take the train on to Heidelberg to spend the night. The next day we go upon the mountain to explore a castle!

We work our way back to Frankfurt. There are no flights directly from Germany to Saudi so we must get a connecting flight, which is a good excuse to go back to Greece. So, that is where we go! We don't dare simply scoot over to another plane. Why waste an opportunity to visit Greece?

"I know the name of the hotel we stayed at last time, but I don't know how to get there. Maybe I should have made reservations." We walk out of the airport looking around like two lost tourists.

"Ah, you seem confused, lost," says a tall Greek man in broken English. "May I be of assistance?"

"You must be a God-send," I reply. "The Ionis Hotel, we don't know how to get there and we have no reservations."

"It is no problem, my lady. We will be glad to get you there." A shorter man steps out of the shadows. "We will be glad to assist you lovely ladies." They open the back doors of a taxi and encourage us to get in. He speaks Greek to the taxi driver. "He take you to da, uh, what you say square? We will meet you there. The hotel is close by."

"Suzie! Big mistake!" Linda utters as the taxi rumbles down the street.

We begin praying that these two men will NOT be there when we get out of the cab.

"There they are," reports Linda. "They are waiting for us with huge smiles pasted on their faces. What are we going to do?"

Here we are in a country where very few people speak English and these two creeps insist on taking us to our hotel, or somewhere else! It is dusky dark, cold and a drizzling mist is starting to come down.

"We no need you," I try to explain in my own broken English. My head turns from side to side in an exaggerated no. "We know where hotel is," my head goes up and down.

"Es no problem. May I have your bag?" he asks reaching.

"NO! " I boldly decline. There were a few people around and the men step back.

"I insist," adds the short one.

"No! Go away!" exclaims Linda. We turn and bravely walk away, pulling our luggage on wheels.

"This is so scary." I mumble as we walk. We hear footsteps behind us.

"They are following us step by step! RUN!"

That we do and they begin chasing us through the cobblestone streets of Athens. We run at least a block then duck into the next open building. They do not walk by. After a few minutes, I peep around the open doorway.

"It looks like we lost them."

We stay in the building a while longer and sneak out one at a time to meet up later at the hotel. We check in and stay in our room for the remainder of that evening.

"Now I know what you mean when you say,

'Adventure'", says Linda and we both begin to laugh.

"Let us refuse to let that bad experience affect the remainder of our trip," we vow to each other. We did learn a valuable lesson.

We spend three days inside the city limits of Athens and walk so much our blistered feet are hurting!

We are happy to finally touch Saudi sand and the kids are very glad I am back. Paul and Dennis went from London to Switzerland for a few, unscheduled, extra days. I felt bad that Nita had to watch the kids longer than we expected. She insists that all is well, so all in all, I think everybody is satisfied.

I am no longer a bus monitor so I have plenty of time on my hands. Paul and I join a square dance club that meets weekly. We are talking "serious square dancing" with several outfits and big white petticoats. The men all have matching shirts! The dances and calls are simple at first and we enjoy the fun. Soon the calls get more complicated and several people comment to me that Paul is not able to keep in step and it messes them up. I, therefore, politely tell Paul that it is getting too complicated for me and we bow out. They still call us when they need substitutes.

Islam is the official religion of Saudi and no other religion is practiced or allowed. Islam honors much of the Old Testament. Friday they worship and Saturday is a day of rest. Their workweek and school week begin on Sunday. We were cautioned about displaying our religion during orientation; however, that did not stop me from going. Since I worship God all day every day, I certainly do not require a church building. My plan is to designate a particular time each week for organized worship/study with just my family.

"How about your home as a meeting place for worship?" To my surprise, there are others of like mind! "There is a minister who lives at Bechtel and will come one Saturday a month."

We will be deported if we are discovered. I consider the risk and decide it is the thing to do. Seven families join us monthly for worship.

It is against the law to have a Bible in Saudi. "Do not pack a Bible. It will be confiscated by customs." No way am I leaving the USA without my Bibles. I took several and prayed they would not be taken away. God answered those prayers with a yes! The inspectors acted as though they did not see the Bibles even though they were in plain sight.

Once, Twan landed with a popular glamour magazine and the inspector looked at it page by page. He would rip out the pages showing any picture of a pretty girl. He looked at Twan with a devilish grin and handed the magazine back to her with only four or five pages remaining.

"How about Bible classes for the kids?" a mother asks me. "We can call it Monday School." Soon there are twelve or thirteen children coming to our house after school each Monday!

"How about an afternoon Ladies Bible Study?" We form a group for women but decide it is too dangerous to add another meeting at my house. Ten of us alternate homes for the Ladies Bible Study and prayer.

This underground worship is a special blessing. You may think it silly, but what we are doing is a serious offence to the Saudis and Islamic Law. Being deported would be the least punishment we could get. Christians are imprisoned and some die for sharing the Gospel of Christ in Muslim countries.

Chapter 11
He Speaks

"The King is coming!" says Paul. "This is huge! There's going to be a parade!" It is a privilege for King Khalid bin Abdulaziz Al Saud to personally come to the Navy Base and visit.

So much has happened over these last two years. Mark and Jeann Gardner moved into a house across the street with their son, Robbie. Jeann quickly joined in and became one of "The Group"!

When you live in a foreign country where very few speak English, you tend to befriend anyone who says, "Hello" without an accent. The women of our community do much socializing and they spend a lot of time together in "The Group". Everyone's personal life remains his or her personal business. We tend to have one or two close friends and still we enjoy our large group activities.

After one of Paul's evening Saluki dog walks, he comes back with the latest gossip! He is anxious to get home and to fill me in on all the juicy details. Of course, I have to listen. The main problem here is that Paul gets most of the details wrong and I end up with a partial truth. (Isn't that what gossip is anyway?)

"A bunch of HBH kids are stranded in Greece!" Paul begins to pour out the day's gossip. "They are getting kicked out of boarding school because they got caught smoking pot or something!"
We know these kids from their visits during Spring break and our visit in Greece.

"Now Paul, you know they wouldn't just put them out on the street. They can always come home."

"Not this time. Jim and Joan Carol's kids and Dianne's son all got into trouble. They are expelled from TASIS School and will be put out on the street tomorrow morning."

I know the implication of this. In Saudi, one cannot come and go at will. You must apply for a visa and hope that you get one.

"Yesterday (Friday) was a Muslim religious day and you know they're off today too," Paul continues. "All of the 'Big Wigs' are out of the office. This means no one can enter or leave the country. No visas will be issued and there is nothing that can be done about it."

"That's terrible! I imagine the mothers are falling to pieces." I know Joan and Dianne from our fun times together. We are not really close friends.

"They have been crying all day. They say only a miracle will help them!"

That evening I begin to pray. In this situation, there is nothing else to do but pray. I lie awake, praying, throughout the night. Around five o'clock in the morning, I get an answer to my prayer.

"Go to Joan and Dianne and have a prayer meeting." It is a voice only I can hear. It is as if the answer appeared in my head and I know it is God!

"Wait a minute," I thought. "Who am I to go to their house and ask them to pray? Joan is Catholic and Dianne is Southern Baptist."

"Go to Joan and Dianne and have a prayer meeting." The voice is like knowing the answer to a question before it is asked.

"They have never expressed their faith to me." I argue. "I don't know how they will react to my telling them to pray."

"Go to Joan and Dianne and have a prayer meeting."

"I'm not a preacher and I have never done anything like this before. Come to think of it, I have never had this type of conversation before! When did you start talking to me?"

"Gerry Sue, I have been talking to you all your life. You just don't listen! Now, go to Joan and Dianne and have a prayer meeting."

"God? I need details. What am I supposed to say? How do I approach them? When do I need to go?"

"Now! Go to Joan and Dianne and have a prayer meeting."

I know the conversation is over. I prayed, he answered. What else is there to say?

Paul is up getting ready for work. I usually wake up the children and get them dressed for school at this time. This morning I throw on some clothes and yell to the kids.

"Everybody up! Get dressed and go to school. You're on your own today." I rush out the door.

It is seven-thirty in the morning and I am ringing Joan's doorbell. I hope her husband has already gone to work. "Lord I believe. Help my unbelief."

Joan opens the door in her pajamas and robe. I barge in saying, "Get Dianne, quick! She needs to come over. It is very important."

Joan trots across the street, wakes Dianne up and brings her back to her house. They look at me, both wearing pajamas and robes. They know something is up, but they have no idea why I am here or what I am planning to do and neither do I!

I feel so very inadequate. Why has God placed this task upon me? I know it has to be done.

"Sit down." We sit around Joan's little breakfast

table. "Now let's talk about the situation."

"I got the call yesterday," says Dianne.

"Me, too," interrupts Joan. "And they told me..."As they recap what happened, tears are streaming down. They excitedly list all the barriers between them and their children and how, in a few hours, their babies will be put out on the streets of Athens, Greece.

"Only a miracle will help us." (Well, at least Paul got that right!) Then, in silence, they look at me.

"God told me to come over and we need to have a prayer meeting." I am wondering what kind of reaction I will get with these words. Now there is more silence and they look at each other.

Joan sits up from her slumped and defeated position and looks at me in a serious way. The look on Dianne's face that says she is shocked.

Joan says, "Now why haven't I thought of that?"

"Yes," Dianne agrees. "Why haven't we thought of praying before now?" We all hold hands around the little table and begin to pray. More tears come as they pour their hearts out to God. Their children are being cast out in a foreign country and they are miles away, helpless. We continue praying. Then the praying stops. We lift our heads and look at each other knowing, in our hearts, it is done.

"Whatever happens, we know it is in God's hands." I add and I bid them farewell. "Keep me informed."

By noon the telephone rings!

"Hey Suzie, this is Joan. Miracles do happen! The superintendent from TASIS called. He said the kids can stay at the school until Monday. Jim just called and said our passports are stamped. We can leave the country anytime. Can you believe it? Never has anybody heard of getting processed that fast. Dianne and I leave for Greece tonight. I can't thank you enough! Why didn't I think of praying?"

"That's great! Our God is good!" With that I say good-bye to my friends.

Immediately I sing a song of praise and thank God for intervening in this situation. It is wonderful to have a God who directs your path when you listen to his voice.

Chapter 12
Adventure vs. Sightseeing

Women cannot drive in Saudi. We are chauffeured around by Filipinos and Arabs in vans and autos. Weekly the women load up in vans to go shopping in Jubial, it is near and easy to get to.

After shopping, we pick a lovely restaurant to have lunch before returning home.

Every month or so we ride several hours to Al Kobar. It is quite an experience.

"Only in Saudi can you go into town to buy eighteen carat gold by the ounce!" I heard one woman say. Fortunately our husbands are making a lot of money and after a few months we consider going gold shopping. Just a normal trip into town!

After a shopping spree in Al Kobar, Jeann and I have some extra time while waiting for our driver. We sit on a nice, large, outside patio.

"I recently watched the movie, *The Ten Commandments*," I say. "Normally, I do not remember half of what happens in the movies. When I try to tell someone about a movie, it goes from five stars to one in the confusion." We both laugh and I start telling the story.

This time, it is different! It seems like the story flows smoothly from my mouth. Jeann is captivated. She takes in every word I say. She asks questions and I know the answers! It is as if the Spirit of God is right here, revealing to Jeann more than what I am saying. That day Jeann felt the Lord open her eyes to a new understanding of God and His Word.

We spend more and more time together, becoming best friends. We read the Bible and go to the Ladies Bible Study. We even become missionaries on the base. We pick particular days where we knock on doors and ask, "Is there something we can do for you?"

Jesus said, "In as much as you have done it to the least of these my brothers, you have also done it unto me." We put that into practice.

Jeann and I remain close friends. We have laughed together, cried together and shared many wonderful experiences. To find a friendship of this nature is a once in a lifetime blessing.

Every New Year's Eve, a large group of Americans caravan to the Kuwait border to camp out. There is a majestic red glowing sunset and we all prepare ourselves for the hunt. In the dark of night, several vehicles line up side by side. They turn on their bright headlights to shine across the desert and into the darkness. It takes a moment for the eyes to adjust, and then you can see a sparkle, and then another. Lying atop the desert sand is quartz, glistening and sparkling like diamonds. It is so exciting to gather the crystals and nuggets as they flicker in the light. They can be cut like diamonds to make beautiful jewelry.

As spring rolls around, it is R&R time. This trip includes two weeks in Jordan and Egypt. Apparently, I did not learn the lesson of reservations in Athens. I love planning and making reservations for each trip, but I failed to acquire accommodations for our Cairo stay. We arrive in Egypt late in the evening.

"English?" we ask repeatedly.

"No," we receive hostile looks and foreign answers. We find a payphone and start calling hotels.

"American?" We finally find a hotel that speaks English. "Yes, we have a nice suite that overlooks the

Nile! For you a special deal!"

It is very cheap and we head to the hotel tired and happy.

"There is the Nile River," I announce pointing to the wide river as we pull up to the hotel.

"Mom, this place looks spooky!" Twan states, as we look at the three story old dilapidated building.

"Maybe it is nice inside," I am hoping.

"We have for you a three bedroom suite," says the manager. He wears a tall hat with a tassel that dangles and sways as he walks. "Indeed it has a balcony overlooking the Nile."

"NO, it is NOT nice. This furniture is very old and dirty. Look!" I smack the thick heavy drapes with the back of my hand and the dust flies.

"You can tell they were once gorgeous, the whole room was once very nice!" says Paul.

"Maybe a hundred years ago! Now they are dusty, faded and completely worn and they don't match anything," I shoot back. "This entire suite looks like a scene from a horror movie."

"We have to stay the night," replies Paul. "We can look for a better place tomorrow."

"Mama, I'm scared," the kids come to our bedroom one at a time and climb into bed. We all end up sleeping in the same bed. Early the next morning we set out to find another hotel.

We spend a full week in Egypt seeing the Great Pyramids, Sphinx and Giza. We take a train that runs beside the Nile River to Luxor and see the Valley of the Kings and Queens, Luxor Temple, Kornak Temple and many other sights. Back in Cairo, we see the huge gold collection of King Tut. Egypt is fun with so many exciting experiences. Despite the many historical treasures, Egypt is a very poor and dirty place. It is like stepping back in time.

We spend our second week in Jordan and drive all over the country in a rental car.

"This is Mt. Nebo where God allowed Moses to view the Promised Land," I tell the kids as we pull into the parking area.

"What is up with them?" asks Paul. There is a group of young Jordanians approaching our car. I get out and they walk quickly towards me. When they start running my way, I jump back into the car.

Paul visits with them and motions for me to roll down the window. "They see your hair! They have never seen a blond before." I allow them to run their fingers through my hair and they are fascinated.

After visiting the Dead Sea, we drive to Petra, or as close as you can drive. The final journey to Petra has to be either horseback or on camels down a narrow path. We ride horses down the path with huge rock ridges towering on both sides. Petra is also known as the red city. There are beautiful ruins of an ancient civilization. Buildings and living quarters were carved into the red stone valley. Only a few people live there. We spoke to one, a son of the Sheik.

"If you ever come again do not to stay in the government owned rest house, but to come here and sleep with us!"

Two years later, we did just that with Mother and Daddy. We ate with our fingers and had oil lamps to find the chamber pot at night. We slept in a cave on mats and saw a ritual circumcision.

In Aquaba, Jordon, we go down to the Red Sea. We see an old Arab wearing a white robe and turbine headgear on the shoreline and ask, "Can we take a picture?"

"Most certainly," he speaks kindly in pretty good English. I introduce the family.

"You have a lovely daughter," he remarks, pointing to Twan. "I may not be a good looking man. But I am of much worth." A great big smile reveals a large number of whitish and gold teeth.

"Yes?" We do not know where this conversation is going.

"I would value her as well. What would be the dowry required for the older one?" He offers to buy Twan from us. The old Arab wanted to add her to his harem! Of course, Twan refuses and we brought her back home with us!

Back in Saudi, we are excited to tell the others of our adventure.

"We had a wonderful experience staying in one and two star hotels and learning the Middle Eastern Culture. Everyone should try it."

I make the trip sound so great that a few of "The Group" decide to go.

"The trip was terrible! How could you enjoy such a primitive lifestyle? So much poverty and we are lucky to get back alive."

After a few more reactions, I change my recommendation. I suggest, "Stay in four-star hotels and take bus tours." I still consider this a sad way to travel since you never really mix with the average people.

"It's just not right for us to squander all of this

extravagance on ourselves. HBH gives a lot of money for these lavish vacations. I feel rather selfish spending that much money and having it not benefit anyone but us!" I call this a family sit down discussion. "I have thought about it for a long time. HBH gives us $10,000 every time we go on vacation, and the trips we take are much cheaper than that. We've been blessed, and I think we should at least let Mother and Daddy share in our blessings!"

The rest of the family looks on as I continue the discussion.

"From now on, this is the plan: we will stay in cheaper hotels, we'll pay coach fares and that way there will be enough money left to pay for Mother and Daddy to either travel with us or meet us wherever we go! How does that sound?"

With reluctance the family agrees, "Might as well spend it on LoLo and T.J. cause you never let us go first class anyway!"

And we do. Lolo and T.J. travel with us to Austria, Jordan and Thailand. The kids learn my adventuresome streak and economizing comes from Lolo.

In Thailand, Twan has plans to meet her friend vacationing there with her family.

"No way am I telling them we are staying in this dump. Mom, we can't bring them here!" she cried. "It's embarrassing!"

"OK, Mom will fix it." I utter. Therefore, they join us and we dine at our expensive "pretend" four-star hotel.

"It is so nice here, much better than where we are staying," says her friend.

"It is worth every penny we paid for it," adds Twan smiling.

I'm always more comfortable going less than first class for some reason. Putting it bluntly, I'm just cheap.

While we are in Thailand, I have those quartz stones cut like diamonds. The crystals do not have the strength or value of a diamond, even a cheap diamond, but they are lovely. Several I have mounted into rings. I love to tell the story of how I acquired them.

In Bangkok Mother and Daddy join the family. The restrooms are primitive in Thailand. The kids and Lolo go to the "ladies room" which is an eight-inch plastic pipe sticking three inches up out of the ground. The floor is made of white sand. The kids are barefooted and Mother notices the sand around the pipe is yellow.

"Watch out," claims Lolo. "You can catch a disease if you step in the yellow."

"What?"

"PUSSYFOOT!" she declares.

Such comments are common in my family.

In my wildest dreams, I could never imagine getting to travel abroad as I did for these special years of my life. (1979-1983) I touched the ground of twenty-one different countries. I spent a week or more in at least eight countries. I was blessed to return to five of those countries numerous times! What a blessing. It is as though God, once again, granted me a desire of my heart!

As I write about these marvelous adventures I think about how truly blessed I have been. I also feel a special bond with those whom these adventures took place.

God continually rains showers of blessings on me.

Chapter 13
Sinking In the Persian Gulf

"I want to take you to a special place," says Paul. He sounds like he has something up his sleeve. He has been acting rather peculiar this week.

"You know if one of us were gone, life would go on," he says as we walk out of the residential section of the base.

"You mean gone, like in dead?"

"Well, I mean like, no one lives forever, not that either of us is going to die anytime soon," he says thoughtfully.

We go to a remote place on the base. No one is in sight and there are warehouses that look abandoned. Paul insists on wearing cowboy boots all the time. He thinks he is fooling everyone into thinking he is a Texan. His steps echo as his heels hit the walkway and we walk between the concrete block buildings.

We step out into an opening, he points out across the waters.

"There's the Persian Gulf," he announces.

There is no real beach. The bank is a concrete retainer wall, probably for ships to dock. It is too steep to reach the water, and why would I? There are globs of black sticky crude oil which takes forever to get off skin or clothing.

"Come on," says Paul. There is a long concrete driveway leading down to the water. "It's a boat ramp."

"It gets steeper and I bet that green moss or slime is slippery," I caution.

"No problem. Come on, I'll catch you if you fall." The closer we get to the water the slicker it gets.

"Paul, there is nothing to hold on to and cowboy

boots are not made for this." He starts slipping about three feet up from the water. With his arms wind-milling around, he reaches for me.

Thank goodness, I am smarter than Paul is and I wore tennis shoes. I step back.

Well, down goes Paul sliding down the ramp with those pointed cowboy boots pointing to the sky. First, the boots go into the water and then Paul, lying on his backside. He slips into the water as smoothly as going down a water slide, a concrete water slide which gives his head a crack when it hits the bottom. He goes limp, slowly slithers out into the water, and just lays there. His unconscious body is floating and his head is out of the water, teetering on the concrete slant. He slips farther down the ramp until only his nose is above the water, then with a wave of the Persian Gulf he launches out to sea, sinking just below the surface.

This is my perfect opportunity to get rid...of Paul...permanently. I only I have to stand at the water's edge and hold his head down. He is as limp as a dishrag and it will be easy. I grab his thinning hair.

"See how simple it is? Just hold the head under." I say to limp and lifeless Paul. "On the other hand I can easily raise your head out of water and you might live." I pull his head up, enough for his nose to surface. At this point, I have to do a little soul searching. Am I actually considering it?

"We are all alone. It will definitely look like an accident," I say slowly letting his head slip back under the water. "Think of it as a permanent baptism. Your life is in my hands and I like it!"

I am gazing into the water when I hear voices.

"Lady, are you alright!" Two men are pedaling toward me in one of those stupid little paddleboats.

"Help, we need help!" I yell and reluctantly pull the hair to raise his head. The men peddle/paddle harder which makes more noise and it churns the water behind them, without making the boat go any faster.

The men come in for the final rescue and drag Paul up on the ramp. He is still out cold with his sopping cowboy boots still pointing to the sky. In a few minutes, he starts moving and coughing and then starts looking around, wild eyed.

"What happened?" he asks.

"I saved your life is what happened!" This is something I have to remind him of every now and then.

Several times, I wished I had done it, but I knew it wasn't right. Don't know how life would have been if I had.

Chapter 14
Marvin Miller

"Your sister is calling!" says Paul, handing me the phone. "She sounds upset."

Phone calls from the States are few and when there is one, it usually means bad news.

"Perry?" I ask.

"It's Marv, he's dead!" She is not exactly crying but her voice sounds strained. "He was 40 years old and too young to die."

"What happened?"

Perry Jo met and married Marvin Miller, her skydiving partner, in Abilene, Texas. With two boys, Arden, Jeff, and daughter, DeDe, they moved to Winona and added another daughter to the family, Marlee. Marv was on the school board with my brother Mitch and active in school activities. He enjoyed "running the chain" (measuring for first downs) at the high school football games.

Marv was an electrician in the Air Force before he worked for Xerox. He donated maintenance work at the Methodist church and was a challenge to his Sunday school teacher, asking unending questions like a kid, "Why?"

In 1981, my brother-in-law was a marathon runner and ran at least 10 miles a day. Slim trim and muscular he was a picture of health, or so we thought.

"He said he was tired," exclaims Perry. "He laid down for a nap and an hour later, Dede tried to wake him up. My sixteen-year-old daughter will have to live with this the rest of her life," Perry went on. "He wasn't breathing. We tried everything. Mitch came over and did CPR but he was gone. Dr. Andrews said it was possibly his athletic heart. His heart rate was slower than normal and maybe it just slowed down to a stop."

We talk for a few more minutes and I say, "I'll be there as soon as I can." These words I soon regret. He is dead, end of story. I cannot change it. What good will it do for me to travel half way around the world to... do what?

"Paul, Marv is dead! My going home will not change that. And, I will not make it any easier for anyone. Perry will understand."

"Suzie, its family, book the flight. We will be fine." So, here is Paul, raised without a family, telling me how important family is. "Your sister needs you."

"But I feel so empty inside," I plead.

"Go. It will make you will feel better."

I really dread this trip. My efforts to back out fail. In my mind, facts are facts.

"I have applied for the exit visa," Paul says. "It may take a couple of days."

"The funeral is in a couple of days. What's the use of going to Texas after the funeral?"

Marv's funeral is going on in Texas while I am changing planes in Jordan. It will take two more days of travel and I will lose another day, crossing the International Date Line, before getting to Dallas. I show my passport to a Middle Eastern man in uniform standing at the turnstile.

"The reason for your travel?" He asks the same question hundreds of times a day. The answer he wants is "Business" or "Pleasure" I doubt if he even speaks English.

"I am going home to my loved ones, and mourn the death of my brother-in-law and good friend, Marvin

Miller."

"I am sorry for your loss," he gently hands back my passport. "May God be with you."

The flight goes from Jordan to Austria. Twenty-thousand feet above the Holy Land, I have the most wonderful experience in my life.

I am so stressed about this trip. The first leg of the flight went OK, but I really need to relax. For me to relax means to pray. I lean my seat back, the four inches it will let me, hear the whining jet engines and feel the floating sensation of flying. I look out the little window and see the giant silver wing in front of me. It seems to be ever so slightly waving as we cut through the air. I look down to see desolate mountains and endless sand. I know there is life below, but at this altitude, you cannot see it. It is awesome to think much of the Holy Bible actually happened down there. What is so sacred about the earth below?

I close my eyes to meditate on this.

This is hard to believe....but it did happen.

I see a bright white cloth spread out and draped over a throne, creating a silhouette. I cannot directly see Him, under the cloth, but I know it is God sitting on His throne.

Marv appears, standing to His side and wearing white jogging shorts. He looks at me and I recall the little crooked grin he would often exhibit. This grin is different. There is a look on his face of unexplainable satisfaction and contentment. In fact, his countenance is one of joy and self-satisfaction. I can quickly tell Marv is glorified!

"Well, can you believe this?" I begin lecturing, even fussing, right away! "Marv, I am furious with you! Why did you go and leave Perry here to mourn? I wish it had been Perry Jo who died. Then she would not have to go through all this sadness. You would be sad. It would be easier on me to see you hurting than to see her ache." As I am raking him over the coals, I realize his thoughts are speaking to me.

"You silly girl, don't you know everything is OK. This is no earth shaking matter." He is standing, grinning, his arms folded across his chest and leaning backward with his back arched the way he always stands.

Marv looks over at God and smiles. Then very calmly and slowly he says, "Suzie, Perry is OK. You will talk to her. There is no reason to be sad. There is no way could I be happier. Anyway, why would y'all be sad?" It seems that as he talks, he beams with contentment and is very relaxed. Sometimes the words go in my ears and sometimes it is only thoughts, without words. Nothing is hidden. As we have our conversation, Marv looks over at God and smiles with a type of pride. Without words, Marv says to me, "Everything is clear now. I know what true contentment is!"

As we are talking, God verbally says, "Marv, you know Jim Brown is here and so is your Dad." Marv stands there and slowly nods his head, "Yes, I'll see them."

In a second, he asks God, "What about Roy Dunkle?"

"Yes, he's here, too."

"I want to see him." Then Marv fades away. When he returns he stands there so joyful and says, "Suzie, you have no idea how smart God is! It is unbelievable the knowledge God has. He knows everything! There is no question that God can't answer. He has all the answers!"

"Well, Marv, of course I know, we've been trying to tell you this all along."

"We looked at the starving people in India and they're not unhappy and hurting the way people think they are." Marv is so excited to have an answer to a question that once haunted him. "They're exquisite, and much more cultivated than people you know. You see, they have unseen beauty. They are meek and humble and their dependence is on God. These are God's peculiar and special people."

As Marv explains some of the things God revealed to him, he looks toward God and smiles, then he looks back at me with thoughts saying, "See, now I know all the answers. God Himself is showing and explaining every question I've ever had."

Marv could not see our sadness and he could not understand why we would be sad.

God is giving Marv all the answers and he takes pleasure in each conversation with God. Now, he is finally knowing and seeing God face to face. Marv is the lucky one in this situation!

As quickly as they came, they were gone. I am back in the plane, sitting in my seat, expressing my emotions. There is a Polish man sitting beside me with a look of concern. I am laughing and tears are streaming down my face.

I ask, "Did you see them?" I half expect him to say he did. The presence of God is so real I think or hope everyone on the plane could see it or feel it.

"These are tears of joy!"

He looks at me very puzzled and in his Polish accent says, "I sink (think) I don-know what you mean!"

I know there is no use in trying to explain.

While waiting for my next flight in Vienna, I realize there is no use to try to explain this to anyone! Nobody will believe it, in fact, I do not know if I believe it myself.

I decide not to tell anyone about my vision. I will just say that I know Marv is happy. My intention is to simply comfort the family.

My sister, bless her heart, meets me in Dallas. We embrace and cry.

My first words to her are, "Marv came to visit me on the plane, he is happy, and he knows all the answers now!" God made the words fly out of my mouth! Perry looks surprised. (So much for the big secret.)

"My only prayer was that God would answer all of Marv's questions and show him, His way. You are an answer to that prayer!" Perry exclaims.

"Maybe this is God's way of letting us know that Marv is with Him so there is no need for us to worry. Or, maybe it was to show me how wonderful Heaven is?" I start to talk more, and then I realize Marv's message has been delivered. There is no need to continue.

Now it is a matter of loved ones getting over the sadness and the loneliness of losing him. I personally have the joy of knowing:
1. Marv is in Heaven.
2. Marv loves Heaven!

A funeral in Winona means a week of feasting for family and friends. A long running custom is to stuff the sadness out of bereaving families with casseroles, roasts, fried and baked chicken, ham, green beans, potatoes and at least a ton of desserts: cookies, cupcakes, pies, fried pies, and cakes.

"What more can I say?" We are sitting around with our plates half eaten. "God is Love. Praise the Lord. Halleluiah   Jesus is the answer to all our problems. Thanks be to God for his unspeakable gift!"

"Suzie," says Mother. "It is nice to be positive, but

there is a time for sadness." Everyone is looking at me as if I am crazy. "You seem to be rejoicing because Marv is gone."

"Something happened to me as I was flying over the Holy Land." I tell them the whole story. There is a short silence and a few sniffles.

"The Bible says no one can look upon the face of God. That explains the veil." Mother has been there with her own death experience. "Marv could not understand or see sadness because, in Heaven, there is no sadness! And, God has all knowledge and we all know how much Marv wanted answers."

The air lifts, as the whole group seems to relax and start to ask questions. The questions they ask make it clear they want details.

"Who are Jim Brown and the other guy?" ask Mitch.

"Roy Dunkle," I answer. "I have never met nor heard of other one!"

"They were Marv's running buddies," says Perry. "Both are dead but apparently not gone! Roy Dunkle was jogging and killed by a hit and run car. Marv was so irritated with God and always wondered why He allowed that to happen."

"Now he knows!"

My family has no problem of saying what they think. Some call it a "Shamburger thing." If they think I am full of bull, they will tell me. If they are not sure, they will find out. The questions they ask are not to disprove my experience, but for their own knowledge. By the time we finish they join me in praising God!

This experience allows me to see how anxious we should be for the rapture to take place. Nothing can be better than to go to Heaven, be with God and have what

Marv has.

I wonder if it was God's idea or Marv's. I do not know why they came to see me, but I thank God they did! Oh well, guess I'll ask them when I get there!

Praise the Lord!

MY FATHER
- Oct 21, 1981- the day Marv, her father, died.

My father was good to me.
When I was little, I would sit on his knee.
He would always make me laugh,
He was the best father anyone could ever have.
Before I was older, I would climb on his shoulders.

He was born in 1941 and passed away in 1981,
He has never (and will never) be alone.
It is like a ball that took its last bounce,
He is with his two fathers; that's all that really counts.
From this day on we'll all miss him,

I'll see him in Heaven which is so true,
Since an angel took him, and will take us too!
The love people give us is so great,
They never have been one step late.
We will all make it through this year,
With lots of help from our friends here!

By Marlee Miller age 14

Chapter 15
Small World

Although we live in Saudi, we spend several of our summers in Texas. The kids have many friends from those summer visits.

One Texas summer, Jerome finds out that his friend, Chad, will be gone for a week vacationing in San Antonio.

"Where is San Antonio?" Nine-year-old Jerome asks.

"It's in South Texas. About 350 miles from here," I answer. He gives me a questionable look.

"A vacation, in the United States?" He looks up with a serious expression. "That's strange!"

"That's what most Americans do," I explain. "Not everyone is blessed enough to explore different countries every six months like we do!"

Three years later another friend, Randy Mingee, invites Jerome for a full week of family camping at Palestine, which is Lake Palestine, Texas.

"It will be good for you. You'll see the beauty of East Texas, and enjoy the whole camping experience. Sleeping under the twinkling starry Texas sky, swimming in the lake and food cooked on an outdoor grill." I leave out heat, bugs, muddy lake water and fish nibbling on you while you swim, no TV, and mosquitoes so big you need a blood transfusion when they are done with you.

"But I have baseball!" pleads Jerome. Baseball is his true love. There are several practices before the game Saturday. After much ado and with his coach's approval, it is decided that Jerome could miss practices that week and I would pick him up on Friday so he could still play ball on Saturday.

It is Friday and Mother and Daddy go with me to pick up Jerome. The thirty-five miles to Lake Palestine is a very pleasant drive. I feel sure my parents enjoy getting out for the afternoon.

We get to the campground with no problem but finding their exact location is another story. Randy's parents told me exactly where the campsite is located, but every campsite looks the same. We drive slowly around the property looking intently for the Mingees and Jerome.

"Is she making gestures at us?" Mother asks. "Look, that lady standing in the back of that pick-up. She is acting strange! See her?"

"She's trying to get our attention." I answer. She is she shaking her head NO, and with her finger over her lips saying, "Shhhh?"

Suddenly I realize who this woman is!

"Mother! That's the gypsy who stole Roy. It's Georgia!"

Roy had not seen Jerome since he was only a few months old. As far as I know, Georgia had never seen Jerome.

"Is Roy here at the lake with her? Has he seen Jerome? Has she seen Jerome? Where is Jerome?" My mind is full of questions as I stop and get out of the car.

"I want to know what is going on," I ask. "Is Roy here?"

As we are talking, Roy walks up! He solemnly speaks about the events of the week.

"We are camping here at Lake Palestine and met a nice couple who mentioned they live in Winona. They brought their son and his best friend, Jerome. When I heard Winona and the name Jerome, I couldn't believe my ears! Could this be my son? When I saw Jerome, I knew he had to be my son!"

Roy is elated as he tells of the experience saying, "I think God has allowed me to spend these few days with my son, which is a dream come true. Please don't tell Jerome who I am."

Can you imagine? Here is Jerome, 7,780 miles from home at a remote fishing lake. Roy is at least seventy miles from where he resides in Longview. The two manage to be in the same place at the same time, not only for a split second or a few minutes, but for five full days. I call that an "act of God" and not just coincidence.

As I look for Jerome, Mother pulls Roy aside and gives him a piece of her mind.

"It has been eleven years and there is something I have always wanted to tell you," says Mother, and she does. I do not know exactly what she tells Roy, but she seems satisfied after the conversation.

I find Jerome, gather his "stuff" and we begin our ride home.

"See these sunglasses? A really nice man bought them for me!" Jerome says. "He was just a stranger, a man at the campsite who really liked me. He took Randy and me for rides in his nice big boat. He even took us into town and bought me gifts. He likes me better than Randy!"

The sunglasses are an expensive brand and Jerome is very proud of them. I remain silent as Jerome talks on and on, in amazement, about the man at the lake.

Saturday Jerome hits two homeruns. It is the first year he receives MVP (Most Valuable Player) of the league!

Neither Jerome nor Roy ever saw each other again after that once in a lifetime experience.

Many years later Jerome had children of his own. I asked him if he remembered the man at Lake Palestine. He thought for a minute. I remember a man who was really nice and bought me a nice pair of sunglasses." I told Jerome that the stranger at the lake was Roy, his biological father. Unbeknownst to Jerome, he had spent five days in the presence of and with the undivided attention of his biological father.

Chapter 16
Getting Back in the U.S. of A.

"I will not go to school in ANOTHER foreign country! I've enjoyed being here, but I want 'a go back to Texas," Twan shouts. "I'll be in high school and I want to be with my Winona cousins and friends."

"We have been over this twenty times. Give it up!" I say, trying to calm things down. "Twan, you are sixteen years old and you've got the chance of a lifetime. You can live in Greece, or even Switzerland, and go to high school. Besides, you already have several friends there. Living in Texas is a NO while we live here! The rest of us aren't ready to go back to the states."

Paul spoke with convection. "I'm not ready to leave, I love Saudi and the job isn't completed. I'm staying until the job is officially over. If you go, you go without me!"

Now that is a threat I can live with. I raised my eyebrows and said a silent, "Thank you Lord."

As usual, Twan's wishes continue to dictate our life.

"Bye Dad," the kids hug Paul and run into the airport.

We travel with friends - Stacy Barber, her brother and her mom. They are like me, returning to America and leaving their man in Saudi.

"This may be our last trip abroad. Sadly, our traveling days are over," I explain to the kids. "I'm glad we took this week to explore London one more time."

The sea breeze feels good as we board a ferry to cross the English Channel going to France. Paris! What could be more fitting? We stopped in Paris on our way in four years ago and now on our way out. We have more fun this time. I have a bittersweet feeling considering I am not yet ready to settle down to the American lifestyle.

"Is this our final eleven hour flight across the ocean?" I say to no one, soaring high over the Atlantic. My mind reflects over the last few years as I look across the aisle to those resting peacefully in their seats.

Back in the U.S. of A.

Life in America goes smoothly! There is no doubt that God is directing our path! A house, which I saw and loved before we left for Saudi, is for sale! The Winona high school principal has left town and his house is on the market! He only wants his equity in the house. This means no closing costs, no closing of escrow. All I have to do is change the names and move in. We jump at this Godsend. Within two weeks, our household storage arrives at our new house in Winona.

It is fun to unpack the things we have missed for four years. We fill the new house with our old "stuff."

Connie's and Jerome's best friends live only a couple of blocks away. Twan is wasting no time letting everyone know that she is back to stay! I am excited. This is an ideal situation, Paul is in Saudi and we are here. I believe Paul likes it just as much as we do. I never discuss my feelings for Paul with the kids or anyone else.

Good ole USA! I quickly realize the luxurious, carefree lifestyle of overseas living is about to change. Somehow, **stress** seems to attach to everything I do.

I have a swimming pool and Jacuzzi built in our back yard.

"We don't really like it," say the kids. However, I enjoy evenings in the hot bubbling massage of the Jacuzzi.

Twan is rebellious.

"What were you thinking, sneaking out of the house at midnight?"

"Dad is in the hospital," Mitch calls. "It looks like a stroke or something. Anyway it is pretty bad both physically and mentally." A few months ago, we were with them on a trip in Jordan.

My father was quick witted, liked to have fun and had the temper of a short-fused firecracker. He was a hard worker and self-employed (except for the Army) all his life. After farming, growing roses, truck driving, raising cattle and running a service station for twenty years, he retired and three years later at age 67 his carotid arteries are ninety percent blocked and he is confused. Surgery keeps him alive and he would later be able to sneak off on his orange tractor and drive to town because he was not supposed to drive at all. Every now and then, good or bad, a glimpse of his former personality would show through. Mother was glad to see him come home and took on the task of taking care of him.

I hire Jimmy Aires, a nice lady, to watch the three kids as I take a two-week trip back to Saudi! While I am changing planes in New York, I call home.

"How are the kids?" I ask.

"I quit! The kids were supposed to come straight home from school and that was two hours ago. I can't handle them."

I call for help. "Mother, Can you keep the kids during the two weeks I'm gone?"

Now I am back and stuck at Dallas/Fort Worth

International Airport waiting for my ride. Twan is supposed to be waiting for me and she is not here. (*Before cell phones*) I wait and wait.

"She left four hours ago," says Mother, and I wait some more. After another hour, I call my house and who should answer the phone?

"I was coming to get you but the traffic got so bad I just turned around and came back home," says Twan.

How am I supposed to react to that?

Yes, life has become a series of major **stressful** events.

In order to help me cope with the problems of life, I begin going to a Christian counselor. The counseling is very good for me. I am reminded that all things are of God. Though we might think certain life events are bad, God sees the bigger picture and is working these bad situations for our good.

Archie Veal is my counselor at Stresscope Counseling Services. Several of his clients and I decide to begin our own Sunday mornings meetings. We call the gathering Love Fellowship. About fifteen of us meet, sing hymns, read the Bible and receive a short sermon. Archie is the main speaker and I deliver the message once a month.

I start a weekly letter to the members of Love Fellowship. Each week I share a few words concerning one of my stressful events. The one page is lighthearted, colorful and shows the good side of "crappy" situations. My intention is to show that we can live above our circumstances and the problems we face.

It is neat how *Suzie News* comes about. I wake up during the night, reach for my pen, and pad. Hurriedly, I write the message. After a few days, I edit, type it up and send out the letter. I artistically insert small figures in blanks. For example, the title might be - - -Do U C A Rainbow? Instead of the word rainbow, there is drawn, a rainbow. The page is full of little drawings in each paragraph.

Everyone enjoys *Suzie News* and people ask me to add others to the mailing list. There are thirty-six letters sent out each week. When I go to someone's home, it is nice to see the week's page stuck to his or her refrigerator.

Note: God gave me these quaint messages for a few years. That was a great time in my life and I loved having God speak to me in that way. Once the messages stopped, I quit writing. I was sad when God no longer revealed himself to me in that way.

Chapter 17
Learning to Listen

"We have no groceries in the house and the gas tank gage shows empty," I am on the phone with my new friend Allie. She is desperate. "I guess the kids will have to ride the bus to school this week."

This is the first time she has ever called me in tears. We have spoken about her alcoholic husband. He is not very reliable. Even though he works for the railroad and has a well-paying job, he does not provide for the family. His biggest concern in life is making sure there is an extra bottle of booze waiting for him.

Immediately my mind starts working. I know the Christian thing to do is to buy them some groceries and give her a little cash for gas. Therefore, I spend my day in town buying groceries and other things I think the Mayberry family might need. This happens to be my shopping day so it works out fine. I put their groceries on the kitchen table and I put my few groceries away.

When my kids get home from school, they are in awe!

"Wow," says Jerome. "Look at this! Mom bought out the store. Wow, thanks for all the good food, this is the best!"

"What happened? Why don't you bring stuff like this home all the time?" Connie asks, happily digging through the treats.

"Get out of there you two," I warn them. "This is for the Mayberry family. They are out of groceries and have nothing to eat."

"They're going to have more to eat than we do," argues Connie.

"I bought these groceries for them. If you like, you

can go with me to their house and help deliver." With that, the smiles go.

Connie looks into the refrigerator and shakes her head. Both decline my offer.

In my next Stresscope counseling session I kind of brag about my experience.

"Deed accomplished; I feel good about myself. I did the Christian thing by helping Allie," I tell Archie.

I am not expecting any reaction, just relaying what I have been doing this past week. Much to my surprise, Archie gives me a startled look and asks, "Did God tell you to do that?"

"What do you mean? I did what any Christian should have done. It was the Christian thing to do!"

Archie begins to expound on the scriptures. He explains that as we live from the Spirit of God, we should always be listening for his voice. Jesus did nothing unless his Father told him to and He waited on God at all times. His disciples often question why he delayed on something they thought he should do right then. The story of raising Lazarus from the dead is an example. Jesus waited three extra days. He did what his Father told him. Several times Jesus said, "Wait."

"Listening is just another way of living through the Spirit?" I never realized that we should stay alert and always listen for his voice.

Archie challenges me to spend the next week listening for the voice of God and obeying it.

I go home and search the scripture. Yes, indeed there is much in the Bible about God speaking and his children hearing. This week, I will begin to make an intentional effort to hear God.

After praying and asking God to speak to me this morning, I think that I should get out of bed and begin the day. Then I decide not to get up but to wait, and listen for God to tell me when to get up. It is relaxing to lie here half-asleep and wait on God. Relaxing swiftly changes into rushing! It turns into one of those mornings where I am going to be late for work at the Scroll Christian Bookstore. They are depending on me to open the store this morning.

Fifteen minutes down the road, I realize the store keys are on the dresser at home. I turn around and speed back down the country road to the house. I round a curve and there is Maudy, a little old black lady, walking from town toward her house. The skinny withered woman walks a lot.

"Stop and ask Maudy if she wants to ride." The thought pops into my mind. I don't even slow down.

Mercy! Could that have been the voice of God? "God, I know I'm supposed to be listening for you but you don't understand. I am going to be late for work. I don't have time to stop for her today."

I wave at Maudy and shoot up a quick "God bless you" prayer. I run in and out of the house and with the store keys quickly head back to Tyler. Five minutes later, I wave again at Maudy as I zip by her.

In downtown Winona, I go by Kay's Grocery and Feed, the main grocery store in town. It is Tuesday morning, almost ten o'clock. I need to be opening the bookstore in Tyler, NOW! It is twenty minutes away, if I am not stopped for speeding. In Kay's parking lot, I see Mrs. Christine Rogers, a longtime member of the Winona Methodist Church. I have not seen or spoken to her in months.

"Go back and greet her." I hear these words.

Can you imagine the mystique? I prayed this morning for God to speak. I vowed to listen for His voice. Now I think I have heard him twice and, it is not even noon! Can this be?

"God, I don't have time, I'm going to be late for work. I'll call Mrs. Rogers, soon and let her know I saw her in the parking lot. We can get caught up on the latest news then."

I continue my day, arriving at the bookstore a few minutes late, if you consider twenty-five minutes as a few.

Throughout the following days, I continue to listen and I get a little better at obeying. However, when I don't obey, the mountains do not tremble and all outward appearances remain the same. He speaks in a gentle way telling me specific things to do. It is another way God leads us, through His voice!

"Did you hear about Maudy?" Perry asks. Maudy lives across the road from Perry. "Last Tuesday, she was mauled by several dogs."

"Really?" I am shocked.

"Walking home from town and she was attacked by at least three dogs. An ambulance had to take her to the hospital. She is all bruised up."

"When did it happen?" I am hoping to hear late in the afternoon or at night.

"It happened Tuesday morning, around nine-thirty or ten. They had to sow her up, thirty stitches."

This news breaks my heart. Why did I pass her by?

"Mother, why are you all dressed up?" I ask.

"I'm going to visitation. Christine Rogers is at Burks Walker Funeral Home," she says. My face is red, on fire. "Suzie, are you all right?"

My mouth is open gasping for air. I have to sit down. How can this be?

"How can I be so stupid?" I ask. Mother looks at me wondering what is going on. "I am devastated God has spoken and I heard, but, I did not obey."

I call Archie in tears and tell him rapidly what happened.

"Calm down and come to my office."

I walk into Archie's office with swollen eyes, "I failed myself and God. I am seeking God to the best of my ability only to disobey his instruction when He speaks. Because of me, dogs mauled Maudy and poor Christine is dead. Boo-hoo-hoo, woe is me."

In a pastoral voice, Archie begins, "Let's talk about this. You say you prayed to hear God's voice and you did hear God's voice." I nod my head. "You know He spoke to you." Again, my head goes up and down. "True, you didn't obey when He spoke about stopping for Maudy. Have you stopped for her before?"

"Yes, I've stopped many times and asked her if she wanted a ride. She walks that road all the time."

"Does Maudy always accept your offer to take her home?

"She has a few times. But, usually she likes to walk."

"If she refused the ride she would have been attacked by the dogs anyway. You should not feel responsible for Maudy's plight that day."

"What about Christine? What is my lesson here?"

"There is a cost for not listening to God and a reward for acting when we hear. You missed the privilege of visiting with the old lady. You both missed words of friendship and the joy that comes when Christians greet one another."

He continues, "Suzie, before you beat yourself up too bad, think about the many years that you and most other people fail to listen to the voice of God. He doesn't give up on us."

"If I had stopped for both Maudy and Christine, there still would have been plenty of time to open the bookstore. I didn't have my first customer until eleven-thirty."

"God will not ask us to do anything without providing the time and energy for it to be done."

After the Godly counsel, I feel better. These lessons are a great leap for me in my Christian walk. I vow to continue intentionally listening for God's voice and acting on what I hear.

"And then there is discernment," adds Archie. "What looks like the Christian thing might not always be so. Does the voice you hear belong to God or you? Sometimes good intentions can have bad results."

"What do you mean?" I ask.

"Take the family you helped with groceries. Is it possible that if well intentioned Christians stopped supplying the family with groceries and gas money, her husband would realize if they are going to eat, he must do the job himself?"

"That's a good question. Was I a helper or an enabler, by providing for the Mayberry family that day?"

Until we learn to listen and recognize God speaking to us, it is good to do the Christian thing. When we are conscious of His voice, we should listen for it and act on what we hear. God will not keep us guessing. He is there continually speaking and we should always be listening.

I thought about my children's faces, the smiles and excitement when they saw all the good food I bought for Allie; I realize it is time for me to make a change. From now on I will bring home better foods for us! No, God did not tell me to do that, it was just the Christian thing to do.

Chapter 18
New Lifestyles In America

Paul fulfills his contract and he returns to Texas in September 1984.

"The Lord giveth and The Lord taketh away, blessed be the name of The Lord!" I shrug my shoulders and quote the Bible. Paul's return is strike one. Strike two and three, are the two investments, I made years ago. They turn upside down! We lose $40,000 in the blink of an eye!

"I agree with Paul," Mother adds. "You have a wrong attitude. It is bad enough to lose the money. You should be at least a little upset. I have seen you more upset over burnt toast."

"It was money we were not using, an investment. Some pay and some lose. Besides it has been paying us 19% monthly for three years!" I say, "We will survive. I've no doubt of that."

"It was money I planned to use to make life better for us," says Paul, still shaking his head.

"I'll look for a job today," I say. While I am getting ready the doorbell rings.

"Are you Suzie? My name is Marianne Adams. I'm a rural mail carrier for the post office in Winona." After short small talk she continues, "Each carrier is allowed to pick their own substitute mail carrier. I want you to be my sub! With my seniority, I will take off every Saturday and any other days I might choose. I will probably take off on Tuesdays because that is "marriage mail" day and one of the hardest days to deliver. I will most likely call in if it's cold or rainy."

Marianne warns me, "Rain, snow, sleet or hail, nothing will stop the U.S. Mail. You will earn your pay! Fae said you are a Christian and might be interested."

Fae had no idea that I needed a paying job.

The U.S. Postal Service is one of the better jobs in East Texas and probably one of a few jobs in Winona. It is a guarantee, I will work every Saturday and most Tuesdays.

"You are a Godsend!" I tell her and that visit is the start of a wonderful friendship.

I continue to volunteer at the Christian bookstore on Tuesdays and Thursdays when I am not carrying mail. One Monday, I feel God urging me to go to the store and work. It feels a little strange going into the store early and on an unscheduled day.

"Where is Brenda?" I ask Debby, the storeowner.

"Brenda called this morning. She was thrown off a horse yesterday and broke her leg!"

"When will she be back?"

"She's not coming back. She resigned her position as manager."

"Wow! If Brenda's position is open, I would love to be considered. The manager is off on Saturdays, and that works out perfect with my post office job."

Without hesitation Debby says, "You're hired!"

When Marianne needs me to work, I get volunteers to take my place! I believe God orchestrated these two jobs especially for me. I got both of these jobs without completing one application for employment!

A job description at the Christian bookstore is providing personal service to our customers. If we detect a need, we might suggest an appropriate book or pray with them. It is more than a job; it is a ministry that I love.

While managing the Scroll Bookstore, God sends a young man my way. Glenn Lauck is the son of Dr. Robert

Lauck who was a prominent gynecologist in Tyler during the 1960's. Glenn is very courteous and polite. After a short conversation, I can tell he has special needs. He is a troubled, sensitive and fragile person. He loves music and after a few visits, I offer him a volunteer position in the music department. He comes several times a week. Gradually Glenn begins to be a part of my life. He meets my family and is included in many of our big family gatherings.

"There is not much demand for an office manager around here," says Paul. "I have filled out applications but most places are downsizing."

"The bank account is shrinking." I have an idea. "We can rent this house for more than the payments. It will supplement our income and we won't lose the house."

"We have to do something. We can't live on what little you are making and the savings is about gone," adds Paul.

In order to save our house, we move out. It soon rents for $150 a month more than the payments. We move to a cheaper rent house in Tyler. Now we have the two rentals we had accumulated before leaving for Saudi and rent from the farmhouse, plus the extra money coming from this house in Winona. We are able to survive financially.

"I got a job," declares Paul. "I am a professional bug killer."

We get another car so Twan and Connie can to go to Winona High School. I transfer Jerome to a middle school in Tyler. He does not like that at all.

Stress in America is taking a toll on me.

One day Paul walks up to me and starts to give me a kiss. When I realize he is there, I start screaming, "Get away from me. Don't touch me. Go away!"

The reaction to Paul's physical affection toward me is unexpected. It came upon me suddenly and I have never reacted so strongly that I could not to control myself and now I have lost control.

I am crying and screaming at Paul.

Twan comes out of her room scared to death.

My knees buckle and I am sobbing so hard I am unable to speak. Paul does not have a clue. He and Twan drag me to bed where I remain for the rest of the day. The following morning I feel better. I realize what happened.

My feelings came to the surface and I could no longer hide them: Not to myself, not to Paul, and for sure not to everybody else. I try talking to Paul in a calm way. The words sound meaningless and hollow as I attempt to gently convey my feelings.

What I want to say are the same words I heard Roy say, twelve years earlier. "I don't love you. I never loved you. I can't stand to be around you." This hurts Paul immensely.

The sudden breakdown is a surprise, not only to Paul, but to me as well. I have always been able to control my negative emotions. This explosion is evidently a buildup of eleven years of resentment.

"I am moving to the farmhouse," I tell Paul. "I will move the renters out. The kids can choose where they want to live."

Two weeks later Jerome and I move to the Winona farmhouse. Twan and Connie stay with Paul. They like the freedom from me as well as city living. After a couple of months, the girls move in with Jerome and me. Paul moves into a small cottage in the Winona area. Within a year, he gets a better job and moves to Phoenix, Arizona.

Paul files for a divorce. In the property settlement I get the two small houses leaving me with a total of three, (the farmhouse was mine from the first marriage). Paul keeps the big house with the swimming pool. God impresses on me to relinquish all of the "stuff" we acquired overseas to Paul. We each keep a car.

When people learn we were divorcing, they admit they were not surprised. Although I am relieved, I was surprised. I felt sorry for Paul because he did not realize what happened nor could he understand why. I do not feel guilty for leaving him because I was a very good wife. He now has three children, which he loves, and he had eleven good years of my life. He was a good husband, a good provider and a good father, as well. Too bad, I could not stand to be around him.

As I look back over those years, I realize during the easy times, when there was money, with our lives focused on the children, it was easy to suppress the bad feelings I had for Paul. However, when the times got rough and the children were older, I was not able to cope. I am sure many of you will see me as a fair weather friend! I think you will find I have a tendency to latch on to disenfranchised and problematic people and try to help or change them into something better. Sometimes I have to give up.

I Give Up!

I guess the time has finally come.
To cease laboring for God!
I've worked and strived to win the race,

The long weary path I've trod!

I am relieved of this burden,
I cast it all on the Lord.
My true self a failure
All MY works I discard!

My independence is considered mature,
In the eyes of those around!
But God's ways are opposite,
Which makes the following words so profound.

BECOME DEPENDENT ON GOD
THEN MATURING YOU'LL BE!
LET GOD DO YOUR LABOR
YES, THIS IS THE KEY!!
God through you, mighty He will be.
Again, I say, this is the key!
      Suzie

The Accident
Part 4
Ron's View

"Get up and keep quiet." Ron looks down at Cleo. It is six feet from his eyes to hers.

"Ariff," a high squeak comes from Buffy, the other pup.

"That means you too." Ron warns the dogs again as Elizabeth rattles ice chips into an ice chest.

It will be three hours until sunrise on this cold crisp day.

This Texas visit was to celebrate Ron's mother-in-law's eighty-ninth birthday! The event blossomed from a family birthday party to an elaborate community reunion.

The Winona Methodist Church was full of friends and family. Leola's three children, eleven grandchildren, and a host of great grandchildren joined in the surprise gathering.

The real icing on the cake was unveiling the brass plaque for the Church's beautiful new prayer room, "Dedicated to Leola (Lolo) Shamburger." What an honor, and what a total surprise it was for her! Leola is a true saint and everyone who knows her has no doubt.

"This family celebrity stuff is foreign to me," says Ron. "Just look at all these people!"

After the celebration, Elizabeth starts loading up the Caravan. For five days, she has put things in, taken things out, rearranged and added more.

"Looks like we are ready," says Ron and slides the side door open for the dogs. Buffy is cocked and ready, always trying to be one up on her mother, Cleo. She watches and as soon as she thinks she can fit through the opening door, she jumps.

"Yelp," says Buffy as she falls and rolls back.

"Not so fast," says Ron. "Let me help you two." He gently picks up both dogs, one in each arm and lays them upon the doggie bed he made for them.

"1500 miles and we are back to Scottsdale, Arizona," says Ron starting the motor.

"Wait! My jewelry!" As always, Elizabeth left something and had to go back. This time it was her jewelry and jewelry is important. Ron's hands are on the steering wheel and he looks at his big gold rings. He shakes his wrist to feel the heavy gold identification bracelet. Lastly, he checks on the gold chains hanging inside and outside his shirt. Ten minutes later in the cool, still of night, Ron sees Elizabeth running back to the van. In one hand, she holds today's jewelry and in the other is a bag, holding the rest of her investment.

"Mission accomplished, this time for sure," she says. "Let's pray."

As soon as they roll onto Interstate 20, Cleo jumps into Ron's lap. There she rides until the next stop.

"We need gas," says Ron.

"Yes, and Buffy is ready to burst," replies Elizabeth.

On their second stop, the sun has risen behind them and a new day is in the making. Ron gasses up and takes the dogs for exercise and a pee break. Elizabeth goes inside and grabs a snack for them all.

"It seems to be getting colder since leaving East Texas." Elizabeth shivers as she slips back into the van and closes the door.

"That was over six hours ago and you are right. They must have had a cold snap here." Ron says as they pull back onto the Interstate and resume a comfortable seventy miles per hour.

Traffic is moderate and seems to be moving right along. The bridges are mostly clear, with occasional ice patches. A huge red dually Dodge Ram pickup passes them.

"You Texans don't know how to drive in cold weather," Ron complains, as the truck quickly moves on ahead in what could be icy conditions.

"Go ahead," Cleo says to Buffy. "I'll stay in the doggie bed."

Buffy hops out of the doggie bed and takes lap duty, moving onto Ron's lap.

Elizabeth sees a shiny black reflection on the surface of the bridge ahead. It is black ice. Ron lets off the gas and clenches the steering wheel.

Somehow, the monster red truck has spun around and is coming straight towards them.

"Don't touch the brake; just try to get into the other lane!" Elizabeth yells. Quickly the sound of metal crunching breaks the outside silence. Elizabeth and Ron lunge forward as seatbelts jerk them to a stop and airbags explode smashing both of them in the face and chest. Everyone in the van feels helpless. They are tossed about like stuffed animals. When all stops, the dash is lying in Elizabeth's lap. The white canvas of the airbags deflates and the powder accelerant is settling. For a second all is dead still.

Time seems to stretch and contract. A minute seems like an hour, or a second, it is hard to tell.

"Wake up! Wake up Elizabeth!"

"Let me help you," someone assists Ron and he gets out of the Caravan. The driver door is gone. He stands dazed, holding Buffy in his arms. He is shaken up, bruised and in shock from all this.

"Cleo!" Ron yells. "Cleo," he calls again trying to level out his voice, hoping to see Cleo running to him.

"I love my dogs more than I love most people, especially Cleo!" Ron has said this a hundred times. It is a true statement, considering Ron is not a people person. His narcissistic personality compels him to judge people. Ron lives mostly for the dogs.

"This your van?" asks the wrecker driver who got there as fast as the ambulance.

"Yes," affirms Ron. He looks over to see a medical team working on his wife. "Where is Cleo? There is another dog. I can't find her."

"Sorry sir, she didn't make it. The dog is still in the vehicle. Don't worry though; we will take good care of her. We have dead pet experience. Here is my card."

Ron held Buffy tight. She survived the crash because she was safely tucked in his lap.

Ron watches helplessly as the Volunteer Firefighters and Emergency Crew extract Elizabeth from the van. Her side took the main blow of the crash. They place her on a litter and roll her to the ambulance.

"You're the husband?" someone in authority asks.

"Yes, is she going to be OK?"

"We do what we can. Mitchell County Hospital in Colorado City is a Critical Access Hospital. We need to get her there as soon as possible."

Ron begins sobbing and clinging to Buffy.

"Come on, bring your dog, we have to go," called the ambulance driver.

Ron turns to the wrecker driver. "We have to go. I

am depending on you to take care of Cleo."

"Don't worry," said the wrecker driver. "Cleo has gone to Heaven." He reaches out and pets Buffy. Buffy does not like the smell of the driver. She decides not to bite or bark at him.

Buffy recognizes two words, Cleo and Heaven.

Mitchell County Hospital staff does the best they can. However, they are unsuccessful. Quickly the medical team heads further West down Interstate 20 to the next trauma center.

While waiting, Ron uses his cell phone to start notifying family of the devastating situation. He knows only to tell everyone that it does not look good. She is probably not going to survive.

Ambulance sirens are loud as they finally arrive into the emergency entrance in this next attempt to get some help. Midland, Texas is a city seventy-nine miles west of the crash site. The hospital there is small, however, somewhat larger than the first one. There is little time left to save Elizabeth. Having already received notice, the emergency staff is prepared and waiting as the ambulance arrived. Did they get there in time?

Elizabeth's arrival at the hospital started a chain of reactions. Preparations for Emergency surgery were underway. Elizabeth is still unconscious and continually being pumped full of blood. This new blood, however is not effectively providing the necessary answer to her crises.

Emergency room doctors and nurses, a surgeon,

anesthesiologists and others quickly prepare for surgery.

What is the main focus of Elizabeth's problem? Where in Elizabeth's body are these pints of blood escaping? With the clock ticking, everyone realizes time is of the essence. Soon, the internal bleeding must be controlled. They have pinpointed the problem and now know what must be done, so let the work begin!

Meanwhile loved ones are making their way to Midland. They are bringing along with them prayers and hope, while receiving very little encouragement from the medical staff.

Information travels fast! In a matter of minutes, daughters on the West Coast, son in Arizona, immediate family back in East Texas and friends were changing their schedules in order to make a fast entrance into this remote West Texas town. News of the accident and Elizabeth's grave condition issued notice that there was probably not a lot of time left!

Chapter 19
Single Again With Three Teens

Paul remains in the family. He is the children's father and we see him several times a year. The kids love him. As far as I am concerned, we get along much better apart.

"I am forty one years-old, single and a working mom. I can't spend every evening fighting over homework." I sit both Jerome and Connie down and explain our new life to them. There is no use talking to Twan, who is in a rebellious state. I have no control over her!

They take the lecture to heart and from that day forward get their homework done without a fuss. They even make better grades!

God is blessing my finances. I enjoy working at the Post Office and Scroll Bookstore, even though they keep me busy six days a week. I date some and I am enjoying the single life.

Hands Across America

I am dating Sam Daniels and he is making a date. "It is a benefit held across the United States. On Sunday, May 25, 1986, over six million people are going to hold hands for fifteen minutes, forming a human chain reaching from coast to coast."

Perry Jo, Sam, and I load the back of the pickup with our kids and drive sixty miles to the closest hand holding rendezvous point. What fun!

"It's only five minutes until time for the event.

Look at everybody!" Perry notices that over two hundred people are just standing around. "We're all here, but where is the enthusiasm? Where are the directors of this show?"

"They have been pumping this thing up on TV," I say. "It is going to be the biggest group thing ever and now it looks like a dud. We better make a move or we'll mess up Hands Across America."

Perry and I become cheerleaders and start a chant.

"Everybody across the land.

Let's get together and hold hands!"

We get everyone to form a line holding hands. Reluctantly, everyone is following orders. People are holding hands and form a line, East and West, as far as the eye can see!

Someone starts singing.

"I'd like to teach the world to sing in perfect harmony.

I'd like to hold it in my arms, and keep it company."

I'd Like To Teach The World To Sing was written by B. Backer, B. Davis, R. Cook, R. Greenaway.

Hands across America, raises $34 million for charities and gives Coke a nice advertisement.

This Bud's for You

"Who can we help today?" My friend Bud Warren is a man I will never forget. We have great times together. We set out sometimes, simply looking for people to help.

"Flat tire," says Bud as we pull over to help someone on the side of the road.

"I have to get to work or I will lose my job," the

man pleads. "I don't have a spare tire."

"Climb on in." We take him to work. Then we go back, with our jack we remove the tire, take it to Daddy's gas station and have it repaired. We then put the tire back on the working man's truck!

"I'd like to see his face when he comes back and finds his flat fixed."

Another time Bud and I go to one of my empty rent houses to get it ready for the next tenants.

"The carpet is a mess," I say, as we look things over. "We will have two full days of cleaning and painting." The house has wall-to-wall carpet in all the rooms, except the kitchen.

When we walk in the next morning, the carpet is gone! Yes, the house was completely void of carpet and the floors are swept clean. Why anyone would ever want old carpet is a mystery to me. I have to buy new carpet. The house looks so much better that I go up on the rent.

One down, Two to Go

"Mom, meet David, David Domm," Twan says. She is bringing him to the farmhouse to meet the parent. "We are getting married!"

I do not know what they expect my reaction to be. I know Twan. "If your mind is made up, there is no use for me to try to change it. You are both still in your teens, neither of you have a job, and that car doesn't look very reliable."

"Mom!"

"We can make it happen. We'll have a nice wedding," I say and they look surprised.

Within the week, we have a lovely evening ceremony held at my parent's ranch house. Bridesmaids, friends and family from both sides join in the outdoor celebration.

Paul gives Twan away in the ceremony. She looks beautiful in her bridal dress, next to a large purple tulip tree in full bloom. Judge Mitch Shamburger, my little brother, officiates, plays the guitar and sings. Perry has made an exquisite money tree and everyone chips in, turning the tree green with fives, tens, and twenty-dollar bills.

A party reception includes Daddy's fantastic barbeque chicken. We throw rice and send them on their honeymoon. I hope his car makes the twenty-mile ride to the nice motel in Tyler, my wedding present. With a small honeymoon and the tree money, they are set to go.

Two weeks later, they are crossing Texas, New Mexico, Arizona and Nevada. They plan to make a start in California with the help of David's brother who lives there.

Chapter 20
Meeting Ron

"Mark and I are going to Las Vegas for a trade show," My friend Jeann calls, "We're staying at the Hilton. Would you like to go with us? We have a large room reserved with two double beds. You stay with us!"

I am single, 42 years old and looking for some excitement! I buy plane tickets and plan for the late October departure.

"Suzie, do you remember Ron Cole?" another friend, Nita, learns of my plans.

"Yes a little bit," I proclaim. "Didn't he and his wife live on the street behind me in Saudi? They came to a few of our parties and Thanksgiving dinners."

"That's right," Nita agrees. "His wife Madelyn died last year. Ron lives in Vegas. Can I give him your phone number?"

"Sure."

Soon, I am receiving calls from Ron Cole. We talk on the phone daily and make plans for him to pick me up at the airport in Vegas, October 31, 1987, Halloween night!

I do not remember for sure who Ron is, so I get out my Saudi photo albums and find pictures of him. Yes, I am starting to remember him a little. Talking on the phone about Saudi and times past makes us feel as though we know each other. Ron always jokes and says he remembers continually hearing about those mean Murphy kids.

"Suzie!" I hear Ron's voice at the airport baggage claim.

"Now I remember you from Saudi," I blurt out and

he looks at me quizzically. Ron grabs my bag and leads me to his Cadillac. I get comfortable in the leather seat. Leaving the airport, I smell the aroma of smoke, a lingering cigar or cigarette odor. Ron is wearing a lot of jewelry. I suspect he has been Saudi shopping too.

We drive straight to the Vegas Hilton where we pick up Mark and Jeann. We all lived in Saudi at the same time. Mark and Ron actually worked together.

"I know the best Mexican restaurant," says Ron.

The food is not very good, compared to East Texas Tex-Mex, and the flour tortillas have green mold on them. Ron is embarrassed. We all try to make the best of this awkward situation.

"I'll be staying in the Gardner's hotel room," I say.

"Why?" asks Ron. "You are welcome to stay with me. I mean stay at my house. I have two empty bedrooms."

Since we have been talking on the phone for the past few weeks, I feel I know him well enough.

"Why not?" asks Mark. "Just drop us off at the hotel."

In Ron's house, I feel comfortable from the beginning.

Crazy how everyone who travels to the Middle East returns to the States with a load of beautiful brass objects, gorgeous copper pots, ornate wooden furniture with silver, brass and copper inlay. Paul acquired mine in our divorce. Ron lives here in Las Vegas with all the evidence that he spent many years in Iran and Saudi Arabia. His house is a showcase of "the best of the Middle East."

There are only two problems with Ron. (If you call these problems)

Problem one: the cashmere sweater he is wearing

smells like smoke, strong, borderline stinky strong. I have never, will never, and really do not like tobacco in any shape, form or fashion: Except, maybe a distinguished ivory pipe, with a cherry-flavored aroma, at a distance.

Then there is the dust! Yes, all of his lovely tables and the many fine imports on display are covered with dust! It is not my place to mention this so I keep quiet. On the phone, Ron told me how he was cleaning the house every day for my arrival. Well, the house is beautiful and spotless except for the dust. It is hard for me to resist writing messages with my finger on these gorgeous tables! Don't know how that would sit with him. We have a drink and watch the late news.

"It has been quite a day," I say, as Ron shows me to a lovely guest room. There we part for the evening.

The next day we meet Jeann.

"Have fun," says Ron. "Don't spend all your money in one place. I'll be back around five."

Jeann and I explore the casinos. We enjoy the bargain shrimp cocktails more than the one-arm-bandits. Ron told us about a place that makes huge strawberry shortcakes. The best part is they are only 99 cents!

Jeann and I spend most of the following days visiting and sightseeing. What fun it is, exploring and living in the moment.

In the evenings and at night, Ron and I become better acquainted. We walk BoBo, his German Schnauzer, around the greenbelt near his home. During our conversations, I talk of my favorite subject, which is the Bible. Ron listens intently as I expound the scriptures. I love having a one-man audience.

"What about Jesus? Can you go to Heaven if you are not a Christian? Do you have to go to Church to be a

Christian?" Ron asks a lot of questions while we are sitting in a park. Then he adds, "I love your Spirit."

It is time for the Gardners to return to Virginia and for me to go back to Texas.

"Goodbye, Ron. I've had a wonderful time. Now it's your turn to come to Texas,"

"Well, what did you think of Ron?" asks Jeann as we walk through the airport.

"My very first impression of Ron was not the greatest. However, I think we will see each other again."

Time passes and I have gone to Vegas several times. Ron flies to Texas during these months as well. My family likes him and he is very impressed with them. They have gone out of their way to let Ron know he is accepted. He stays at Mother's house when he is in town.

By January, we decide to get married. We plan to move to Vegas and live. Ron is a real estate broker. He doesn't work a lot, and he decides if he is going to support a wife and children, he better concentrate on selling more houses. I am still carrying mail and managing the Scroll Christian Bookstore. I hint to them that I may be leaving.

On April 15, 1988, I fly to Vegas. We dress in black silk outfits. Our destination is the famous *Little Church of the West*, a chapel at the far end of the Vegas Strip. It is a small, lovely and intimate wedding chapel where 50 to 70 couples per week get married. Many celebrities have walked the same aisle as we did.

A British couple is sightseeing at the chapel. They become our best man and the maid of honor. They are thrilled to be involved in an American wedding.

My plan is to quit work and all of us move to Vegas,

but evidently, Ron has other plans. He decides it is best if he moves to Texas. So with that, we fly my sister and her third husband, Ray, to Las Vegas and they drive a large U-Haul truck, full of Ron's stuff, back to Texas for us.

Ron and I ride around Smith County looking at the real estate. We are living in one of my rent houses. I drive up a long steep red clay driveway to the York place. It is a redbrick, two story, older estate home, sitting on several acres of land. I loved the place, with its huge front porch, when my sister and Marv owned it. Even though the yard is overgrown and the trim needs painting, you can see the beauty within. There is a "For Sale by Owner" sign at the foot of the driveway. I have no idea Ron will consider moving into this wooly looking place. When he hears the price of this quaint estate with a large barn, mobile home, and pecan orchard he becomes excited. We close the deal within three days.

We stay at the rent house and spend our days and nights remodeling. What a mess. It is very time consuming and hard work.

Of course, the kids are glad they do not have to move out of Texas.

"I am gaining weight!" I say to Mother.

"Well it is Ron's fault. He loves to watch you eat and then gives you all the leftovers from his plate," Mother explains. "And you put on the pounds." (This is a "Shamburger thing" type comment.)

"I figure since I am laboring so hard, remodeling the house, I should be burning enough calories to keep my weight down."

"Your figure says, 'Wrong!'" adds Mother. We both laugh.

I go from 118 pounds to 130 pounds! Yes, it did not take long for me to become a 44 year-old, short, fat, little lady.

Meanwhile, the bookstore owner decides to sell the store and my job there goes away.

Marianne offers me a babysitting job, keeping Joseph, her toddler son. On the days I do not sub for her, I take her two daughters to their private Christian school in Tyler and keep Joseph until she finishes her mail route. Ron is very fond of Joseph and they become best buddies.

We have lived in the "Big House on the Hill" for three months. We cleaned, painted and renovated the upstairs.

"That mobile home is sitting there empty," Ron points to it as we sit on the front porch swing. "It would be a perfect home for my mother."

Altha, Ron's mom, lives in Northern California. I take off work for two weeks and we drive to Sacramento. We rent a U-Haul trailer, pick up his mom, and bring her back to Texas. Altha and her parakeet lives in the mobile home for a while, but develops Alzheimer's, so we move her in with us.

"There is no cable TV in Starrville." Ron is getting antsy for a place to get a way. Watching sports is a necessity for Ron.

We buy a lake house on Lake Palestine with a cable TV hook up. Ron spends most of his weekends there, watching sports. After I get off work on Saturdays, I pick up Altha, and we join him for the rest of the weekend.

Kids

Connie starts her rebellious years as a junior in high school.

"She is skipping school and choosing some undesirable friends to run with," says Mr. Nickerson, the high school principal. "Something needs to happen."

"Ron is too strict and he is not my Daddy!" Connie complains. During the summer, we decide a change has to take place. I contact Paul, now living in Phoenix, Arizona.

"I need to do something with Connie," I tell Paul. "She is out of control."

'Well I have room and maybe Twan and David can help." Twan and David moved to the Phoenix area from California. We make plans for Connie to move in with him. I drive Connie to Arizona and leave her there to begin her last year of high school.

Jerome is now in high school and doing well. He is quite the socialite and a star athlete. Ron and I are very proud of him. We go to all the track meets, football and baseball games. It looks like he might get a college baseball scholarship.

Chapter 21
Jerome's 18th Birthday

"Suzie, do you know where Jerome is tonight? Is he with Lynn?" Mitch asks. It is one o'clock in the morning and I try to shake the cobwebs from my mind.

Ron and I are at the Lake Palestine house. Jerome stayed at the house, as he has done many times before. Jerome often spends the night with Lynn and his family.

Still feeling sleepy and trying to remember what Jerome's plans are for the weekend, I answer, "Yes, I'm sure they're together, aren't they always? Why, is something wrong?"

April 2, 1991, Jerome celebrated his 18th birthday and is getting ready to graduate high school. Jerome and Lynn Wintters are the best of friends, dating back to summertime baseball days. Throughout high school, they are always together.

Jerome is dating a girl from Tyler named Michelle. Her good friend Janna hooks up with Lynn, which works out perfectly. Especially tonight! Only a few days after Jerome's birthday, they have the House on the Hill all to themselves!

"It is time to really celebrate! We'll clean the house afterwards. Mom will never know there was a party," Lynn agrees with Jerome.

The party includes Jerome, Lynn, and their girlfriends along with another bud, Chris. Chris is set up with a blind date. The girls are spending the night with Michelle. An assistant coach bootlegs the beer for them.

"It is shorter and quicker to go through Winona,"

says Lynn. It is time to get the girls back to Michelle's house.

"No it is faster to hit Highway 271 and go that way," replies Jerome. Jerome and Chris take their dates in Jerome's car and go his route while Lynn and Janna go through Winona where they will meet at Michelle's house.

At the end of the long red iron-ore hill driveway, Jerome turns left and Lynn turns right.

"Fiery Crash Kills 2" from the *Tyler Morning Telegraph*

Winona – Two Smith County teen-agers died in a fiery automobile accident Saturday evening on Farm-to-Market Road 16 East just inside the Winona city limits, a Department of Public Safety spokesman said.

The driver of a 1968 ford Mustang, Richard Lynn Wintters, 17, Sand Flat community, and Janna Rodgers, 17, were ruled dead at the scene by Precinct 4 Justice of the Peace Mitch Shamburger who performed the inquests.

"Wet roads and high speed were contributing factors to the accident," said Trooper Robert Johnson. "It was just after the vehicle crossed the Harris Creek Bridge, sometime before 11:22 p.m. when it is believed the car veered out of control off the left side of the roadway, slid backward and struck a tree."

Johnson said moments later the car either caught fire or exploded. The bodies were taken to Lloyd James Funeral Home, Tyler.

Wintters was a senior at Winona High School and heavily involved in sports as a two-year starting quarterback for the Wildcat football team and a pitcher for the baseball team.

Hank Tipps, head football coach and athletic director at WHS, said Wintters was a "great kid" who will be missed by many, especially his teammates and family.

"We are such a small school and everybody knows each other; they feel like they lost a brother," Tipps said.

Miss Rodgers was a junior at Chapel Hill High School and a member of the high school drill team.

It finally dawns on me that when they call Judge Mitch something bad, like death, is involved.

"There has been a bad accident," says Judge Shamburger. "It is Lynn's car, but we are not sure who was in it. The car hit a tree, exploded and burned up. There are two people in the car. The driver, they assume, is Lynn. But the passenger has not yet been identified"

With this news my heart sinks. The truth is, Pricket Hill is on the way to our house and Jerome and Lynn are inseparable. The only rational conclusion would be the unidentified passenger must be Jerome!

"We'll be right there," I answer.

It seems to take a lifetime to drive the thirty-five miles to Winona. Only my words are spoken, over and over, "Thank you Lord, Praise you Jesus!" This is what I say and/or think every time my mind is idle or stressed. They are words of praise as well as words of comfort. They remind me of God's constant presence and that He is in control.

As we come to the Winona City limits sign, we see a hearse coming toward us. The night is black, the rain is drizzling and to me nothing else exists. Only a hearse, lighted with the dismal wet street lamps, as it silently passes us by. I am not breathing and have to force a deep breath. "Is Jerome in there?"

Again, knowing God reigns and with a tormented heart, I repeat, "Thank you Lord, Praise you Jesus. Whatever is your will, let it be done."

We drive on, past the old storefronts in Winona to the intersection of Farm to Market 16 East. Flashing lights, emergency personnel, fire trucks, Highway Patrol and sheriff cars are everywhere.

"The road is closed," says a deputy in a wet suit, pointing and directing us not to turn. Ron turns anyway and the deputy approaches. "There has been an accident."

"Where is Mitch Shamburger?" Ron shouts. "This is his sister, Suzie, and we think maybe her son was in the accident! Can you help us?"

"MAKE WAY!" shouts the deputy. "Go across the railroad tracks and pull over to the side."

As we pull away I hear the speakers from the emergency radios pop and say, "Judge Shamburger, your sister is here."

Within minutes, Mitch is with us.

"The passenger is a female," he says. "They are both badly burned but you can tell it is a she in the passenger seat. We do not know who she is."

Mitch has the traffic cleared enough for us to pass the accident scene and go home. Lynn's car is totally demolished and still smoldering.

My sister and a few others were there waiting for us at the house.

"Looks like Jerome celebrated his 18ᵗʰ birthday with

a party." Perry exclaims. "I put away the beer cans."

Perry had already begun her investigation. She found Michelle's address and we go to her house, not knowing what we would find.

When we arrive, everything is damp and gloomy. It is two-thirty in the morning and they are all sitting around looking dazed. They know something is wrong. Lynn and Janna should have been there long ago. Now, instead of their friends, it is me with my little group arriving.

"There has been an accident," We tell the four apprehensive kids. They break down with tears and sobbing. After a short while, we take Jerome and Chris home with us.

The next few days are gloomy. Jerome and Michelle have lost their best friends. Melva, Lynn's mother, wants Jerome at her side as much as possible. It is as though Jerome is all she has left of Lynn. Jerome handles this as best as he can and remains close to Melva. "It is not your fault," she tells Jerome, holding him tight.

I take Jerome and Chris to the home of Janna to offer our condolences.

"You are not welcomed here. You have no business here. Leave now!"

We attend Janna's funeral which is two days before Lynn's. The funeral home is packed with school-aged friends, all saddened of their loss. We expect to hear kind and comforting words about Janna.

"This," says the preacher pointing at the casket. "This is what happens when you don't obey your mother!"

The service is a lecture to the audience, filled with things like; "Janna and her mother did not have a good relationship." "Janna was a rebellious teenager." "Don't drink and drive!"

I hear nothing good said about Janna. Not that she will be missed. Not that she is now with the Lord. Not that she had many friends. No, there is nothing nice said about her. "Janna was a bad teenager and continually disobeyed her mother. This is what happens to teens if they don't mind their parents."

The funeral message is so disturbing that several students leave before the service is over. We remain to the end, but feel sorry that Janna's life is memorialized in such a negative way.

Lynn's funeral is the opposite of Janna's.

"Today we are here to celebrate the life of Richard Lynn Wintters."

His mother was his little league baseball coach starting with T-ball. The entire Winona School closes for the funeral. Fellow athletes and friends all rally together to joyously remember his life.

"Lynn is a Christian and we know he is now with our Lord and Savior."

The Wintters are a Christian family and Lynn's funeral is evidence of that fact.

We leave the funeral with our saddened hearts uplifted.

Jerome seems lost the rest of the school year, without Lynn. He gets a baseball scholarship to Grambling University. He is the only white person on the team!

Janna's mother sues us and our insurance settles with her for $35,000.00. I try to get the insurance company to pay Lynn's family, but they say Lynn's parents will have to file their own lawsuit. I approach the Wintters family with the idea and they decline.

"Money will not bring him back," explains Melba.

So ends the sad story of Jerome's 18th birthday party.

Often, life just isn't fair!

Since the funeral, Jerome and Michelle have never talked to me about this event.

Chapter 22
Continued Life With Ron

Being a landlord is a passion of mine. It has been since renting out the little farm house many years ago. Paul's divorce left me owning three pieces of rental property. Throughout the years, I feel God has given me the ability to provide housing for people. These houses are actually a gift from God, paid for by the tenants!

Managing rental property is not easy. It is easy to understand why someone called a landlord, takes on a negative image. It is a business that thrives when times are good and leaves someone searching for a place to live when times are bad. Many renters think the owners are rich and should easily absorb any loss when jobs are lost or someone is laid off. To many, the decision to pay the rent is weighted against tires for the car, paying the electric bill, going to the doctor, or even Christmas for the kids.

Receiving rent on time (or even at all) is a major problem that would be solved if I screened potential tenants. I just do not do it. I usually accept the first people who seem interested in the property. I look over the rental application and maybe call a couple of references.

God sends the people to live in each house. Prospective tenants often come with a hard luck story. I have compassion and faith that all will work out.

"You are a soft touch," says Ron.

I may drop the amount of the deposit or make an exception to help the renters get back on their feet. I have even let tenants move in without paying the first month's rent or deposit! How bizarre is that?

"It makes no sense using the rent money from one house to pay the taxes on another," complains Ron.

To the world, this is ridiculous and I would never

advise anyone to do business in this manner. However, I will probably continue doing it as long as I own the properties and feel direction from God.

Why do I behave in this way?

Is it because I enjoy the stress of not knowing how much rent I will receive each month? Is it because I like cleaning a filthy and sometimes destroyed house after the tenant moves out without paying the rent for the last several months? Is it because I don't want to mess with the paperwork?

No, definitely not!

The reason I do my business in this manner is because I believe God is using me as his instrument in helping people who need to find housing. I may be a terrible businesswoman, yet on the other hand, I am a wonderful landlord, helping people who have problems find a suitable place to live. Over the years, I have had a few excellent tenants and many very bad ones.

My daddy lost thousands of dollars giving credit to people in need at his gas station. "Don't give out more than you can afford to lose," was his policy. God has blessed both of us for this haphazard practice.

"You are a terrible business woman," blurts Ron. "Why would you rent to someone who doesn't even have a job?"

"They have four kids and she is about to have another," I reply. "And he is supposed to start work Monday. God sent them to us."

"God expects us to watch out for ourselves. There will be no house if the bank is not paid!"

"It is time to sell!" Ron always wants me to sell when the renter moves out.

"Ron, it is the nicest rental house we have." Finally, I cave in and with reluctance sell one house.

This conflict did not prevent us from buying two more small houses. We enjoyed remodeling our house on the hill, so we update these houses and gain two additional rentals. This brings us to five properties. I love it! Ron loves the monthly income but refuses to help with the rent collections. He disappears when it comes time to refurbish between renters.

Change In Family Dynamics

Twan and David move to Dallas, Texas, and are pursuing a new dream.

"You are going to be a Grandmother!" says Twan.

"Marvelous," I reply with expectance. "Let's go shopping!"

Eight months later, "I'm on my way!" I rush to Dallas on May 15, 1990. Dalys D'Anne Domm is born, weighing 6 pounds 6 ounces.

"Dalys! She is beautiful and perfect!" I show her off to Nita, our friend from Saudi, who happens to be visiting in Dallas. I am very excited!

Twan and Dalys are released from the hospital and the family moves in with us for a short while. Dalys has to sleep under a special light because she is yellow. Dalys finally gets over her jaundice and is an exceptional healthy baby!

"It's time!" Connie calls. She is married and lives in Mesa, Arizona. Connie gives birth to Sebastian Xavier

Schroeder on January 3, 1991!

"I am on my way! I can't wait to spend time loving on my first grandson!"

Jerome and Michelle have been dating for three years. Jerome attends Grambling State University in Louisiana, for one semester on a baseball scholarship. He then moves to Letourneau University in Longview, Texas, with another baseball scholarship. Poor grades during his second year knock him out of the scholarship. Therefore, I make a bold move and take Jerome to the Marine Recruiting Station. Captain Recruiter promises Jerome, "If you are good enough, you can play baseball for the US Marines." This convinces Jerome to enlist! He is to report for duty in three months so he and Michelle decide to get married between college and Marines!

On August 14, 1993, on a very hot humid day, a beautiful wedding is held at our "house on the hill". My niece, DeDe, takes over details and decorations. Michelle is a lovely bride with a gorgeous wedding gown. Everything is exquisite. Chairs fill the lawn facing a large front porch. Michelle and the wedding party round the house as my brother, Mitch, serenades on the guitar. They proceed up the front steps. Everything is in place.

"We are gathered here today," Mitch continues with the ceremony. Afterward, we take a million pictures and celebrate with family and friends.

Another Calling

As I sit in my little office one evening, the phone rings.

"Hello, is this Suzie?" It is the unmistakable voice of Roy, my first husband! He is quiet and I can tell he is straining to make his words come out.

"Yes, Roy," and anticipating his question I ask, "Are you happy?" Why is Roy calling me? What does he want now?

The question must have caught him off guard because the phone falls silent.

"Well, I have been thinking…" he almost stutters.

"Cat got your tongue?" I continue. "Roy, it has been over thirty years and two husbands since we were together."

He begins speaking in his slow voice. "Yes, it has been a long time. I still remember you and I still love you. Wouldn't it be great if we remarried! I hear I have grandkids!"

"Are you out of your mind? I HAVE GRANDKIDS! None of the kids are named, Eudy." With that, we say good-bye and that is the last time I hear from Roy. He must have been drunk or day dreaming again!

I continue working as a substitute mail carrier, childcare giver to Joseph and a rent collector. Ron, for lack of anything better to do, starts driving a school bus. He hates it, so he quits after the first semester.

"Ron, The lease is up on your Las Vegas house. Now would be a good time to make a move." We have enjoyed our East Texas experience but the gypsy in both of us says, "Move on." Las Vegas is our new desire. We sell the lake property and we lease our "house on the hill." We move everything, including Altha, to our new abode in Vegas.

Chapter 23
Viva Las Vegas

Las Vegas days are good. We find a church and have a few friends. We love the cheap restaurants and the fun of Las Vegas.

A particular special is after midnight, downtown at the Fremont. You can get a nice rib eye steak, baked potato and salad for $3.99! Midnight food is my downfall. Two or three times a week, we wake up in the middle of the night, dress and proceed to our "after hours" dinner. Then it is back home, back to bed, and back to sleep. This new practice is not good on my waistline. I tip the scales at 162 pounds!

Mother and Daddy, my kids, Cousin Lane and Jerry plus countless other friends come to Las Vegas for visits. We love entertaining friends and family.

"I want my prime rib!" begs Dalys. She is now a toddler with teeth. Twan's family visits are fun.

"Let's get ready." We do not wait until midnight to enjoy the scrumptious family feasts of Vegas.

Ron's family is the opposite of mine. I have never met his son, Greg. The week we were married we made a short visit to see his daughter, Cindy. I have not seen or heard from her since. With Altha's Alzheimer Disease, I often wonder if I have ever met her, even though she lives with us!

On August 20, 1996, Alyssa Jade Domm enters the world screaming! She is very vocal. During her first two years, everyone knows when Alyssa is in the room! She is my third grandchild.

Connie is experiencing troubled waters of her own. Both she and her husband are "hooked on drugs." These are very distressing days. Their son, Sebastian (Bash), stays with us in Vegas for a while. Later his other grandparents keep him for almost a year, until Connie finally divorces Jim and gets off the drugs.

"I'll come to Scottsdale and help as much as I can." I do the little things a Grandma can do. Connie struggles through rehab and gets her life back together. She shows strength and makes some good decisions. She and Bash develop a close mother-son relationship! God blesses Connie's efforts, she becomes a great mom and she succeeds in the business world.

Ron's mom continues to live with us. Her Alzheimer's symptoms increase and she is a handful for us to care for.

Even though Perry's husband, Marv, passed away, the Miller family remains close with frequent Miller Reunions. One branch of the family has a large ranch near Payson, Arizona. I am blessed to have the Miller family treat us as their own. This particular gathering is on the Memorial Day weekend. One of the highlights is watching and betting on the Indianapolis 500 Race.

"Suzie, you better go check on Altha." We have joined the clan at the ranch. It is a wonderful reunion with family and friends visiting.

"Suzie," someone yells. "The race is about to start, you really don't want to miss this! And you may want to check on Altha."

I enter the den to see the couch and chairs positioned to watch the race. Everyone is sitting around viewing the

TV with Altha sitting right in front.

"Yes, I do need to check on Altha," I say. Altha has joined the group topless! She has no idea that she is dressed inappropriately. Moreover, everyone acts toward her as though nothing is wrong.

"Altha, could you come to the bedroom with me?" It takes a few minutes to convince her. She finally does and we redress the problem.

"Happens all the time," Ron tells the smiling group.

"We need a place to go," says Ron.

"We go almost every day."

"I mean a vacation or getaway like we had at Lake Palestine. I've always had a second home, a place to escape."

We buy a small place a hundred miles south of Vegas in the high desert of Arizona.

The home itself is nothing special. The big attraction is the vast openness, a dense Joshua forest and a breathtaking view of the Grand Canyon's West Rim. Meadview is in an isolated location with few neighbors. It is a "water haul" area. We have a water-hauling trailer which we pull to a deep well; we put quarters in the slot to fill our tank. We then bring it home and inject the water into an underground storage tank. That is how we obtain all of our personal water! We drive 100 miles to either Las Vegas or to Bullhead City, Arizona, in order to buy groceries.

The location is where the Colorado River runs into Lake Mead. We are twenty-three rugged miles from Grand Canyon West! The mountainous, winding dirt road which leads to the west rim requires over an hour drive. Tour buses from Vegas wind this path daily and there have been several fatal accidents. We use our four-wheel drive Bronco when making the trip.

The scenery is beautiful and the surroundings glow with an elegance that only God's nature can provide. Every evening we sit on our deck and watch the sunset as a panorama of colors spread across the gorgeous landscape. We are blessed daily enjoying the Grand Canyon's "West Rim".

We live in Vegas most of the time. Ron and I take turns escaping to Meadview. When we both go, Altha goes with us.

Chapter 24
Altha Stroke

"Mother needs help." Perry tells me that it is time for the daughters and son to help with Dad. "He is continually declining and caring for him is wearing Mother out." We decided that she and Mitch will alternate staying the nights with him and I would come for a month at a time. On my second trip, in August of 1997, I was in Texas helping when I received a call from Ron.

"Mom had a stroke and she's in the hospital." Ron was in Vegas alone with Altha.

"I'll be there as soon as I can." I returned to Vegas.

Altha was in a coma and unresponsive to everyone except Twan, who came for a visit. Twan was very attentive and kind to Altha. Tears streamed down her cheeks as Twan sang all of the old hymns that she could remember. Twan is not much of a singer, but the gospel songs touched Altha in a mighty way.

"This is no way to survive," said Ron and we made the decision to turn off the breathing/feeding machines. This ended all external life support for her. We said our goodbyes as they "unplugged" her. We sat and waited for the end to come.

Altha did not die. The nurses were amazed. She continued to breathe on her own.

"It has been almost two weeks. She must be waiting to hear from someone," said the chaplain. I called all of her family members.

"Tonight at six o'clock in the evening I will be with Altha. If you have any last words, or anything you want to say to her, please call. We think this may be what Altha needs to make the transition from this life to the next."

At six, Ron's daughter, Cindy, called. In a few words, she relayed what her grandmother meant to her. Then the phone went silent and we waited. The room was quiet with only the regular labored sound of her breathing. Finally, at seven in the evening, her sister, Ogie, made the meaningful call. I placed the phone next to Altha's ear and as Ogie spoke, tears rolled down her face.

"Love you. Goodbye." An hour later, the breathing stopped and Altha moved into eternity.

The following January, my father, T.J. Shamburger, passed away at the age of eighty-one.

Ron's devotion to the Las Vegas house has changed. He allows unpleasant memories to linger in his mind, thus granting those memories permission to bring him into a state of depression.

Relief comes with trips to the high desert and they become more frequent and last longer. We love the place. When Altha was alive, Ron and I would take turns escaping to Meadview. Now we go together, often.

The trips are faster when we take the Corvette!

Ron's pride and joy is a classic Chevy Corvette. He bought it new in 1984. It is now 15 years old and barely broken-in. The polished black enamel does not have a scratch on it. Once, we drove it to Texas and Ron chauffeured my brother in the Winona Homecoming Parade. The sleek sports car has seldom seen the light of day because it sits in our garage, with a custom cover wrapped tightly around it all the time.

Chapter 25
UFO

On one particular occasion, while we are at our "high desert" home, a very unusual occurrence takes place. Ron is sleeping and I am sitting on the back steps. The clear starry night is beautiful. With the howl of a coyote in the distance and a pleasant crispy breeze, I convince myself to stay up. I simply want to relish God's wondrous creation in the stillness of the night.

The news is over so it must be around ten o'clock. March, 1999, while sitting alone outside in the still of the night, I do not expect to see the following phenomenon! Much to my wondering eyes did appear...Not a miniature sleigh, nor eight tiny reindeer!

What is that? It is a movement to my right, perhaps a falling star. No, it's too close and too big to be a star. I turn my head and look toward the sky. Just above a Joshua tree, there is a light hovering over our yard. It is right next to the house. The object stops and I hear, not a smooth sound, but one of a motor making a quiet, yet chopping noise. I continue sitting, staring at it in amazement! I am dazed; my eyes are fixed on the object. After what seems like a few minutes, I decide it is time to tell somebody. I run into the house to wake Ron.

"Get up, Get up! You've got to come see this!" I order him to hurry and go outside with me. We scuffled onto the deck.

"What are you doing?" asks Ron, wiping the sleep from his eyes. He is not waking up well, and he is definitely not interested in my light in the sky.

"Look and listen," I turn to Ron. "You can't see with your eyes closed. See there, what is it?"

Ron finally wakes enough to realize that I am trying to show him something. "What?"

"Ron, the light, the sound, that object. What do you think it is? Right here in the yard." I point above the Joshua tree.

Ron begins to accept what I am saying and the motor changes sound to a higher pitch and proceeds to fly over our house. We dash into the house and go straight to the front door, only to see it quickly speed away. In seconds, it was gone, right before our eyes.

"It was a low flying plane," declares Ron. "You know we are in the air space between Phoenix and Las Vegas. Planes fly over all day every day."

"I know better! I sit out here all the time and I have never seen nor have I heard anything like this before. It has to be some type of flying saucer. I've heard people describe UFOs and this fits the bill."

"Suzie, it is one-thirty in the morning. Good night." says Ron, and shuffles off back to bed.

What an experience! I know I saw something unusual, but I have no proof. Besides, not knowing what it was, and having no witnesses, other than skeptical Ron, I have to mark it off as a strange happening that I had better keep to myself. (Unless I write a book someday!)

Tuesday morning, and back in Vegas, I go to the community swimming pool for a morning of water aerobics. As I approach, someone shouts from across the pool.

"Suzie, have you seen any UFOs lately?" It is my neighbor, Linda.

"Yes, as a matter of fact I have. How did you know?" I shout back to her.

"The news reported UFOs were sighted near Meadview, Arizona. I saw it on TV Sunday and I knew you were at your place in the high desert."

"Wow!" I reply. "I did see a UFO!" *Confirmation #1!*

Fifteen years later, my brother checked out my story!

Confirmation #2!

As reported on the UFO internet sight

Date of Sighting: Spring, 1999 (Exact Date Unknown)

Time of Sighting: Late Afternoon (Exact Time Unknown)

Duration of Sighting: 5 Minutes

Location of Sighting: Meadview, Arizona

Latitude: 35.8 Degrees North (Airport)

Longitude: 114.3 Degrees West (Airport)

Number of Witnesses: Two

Number of Witnesses Interviewed: Two

Weather: Clear Skies.

"The witnesses said that they were sighting in their rifles at a remote location near Meadview, Arizona. The witnesses stated that they hear a high pitched sound and looked to see a large black "stealth-like" aircraft hovering right overhead. The craft had no markings, showed a "heat signature" from the rear-end, had no visible windows, and continued to make a high-pitched sound. The craft approached from the north (Nevada), hovered about 5 minutes, and then rapidly zipped away. The witnesses heard no sonic boom, saw no jets firing when the craft took off and departed towards the north.

Chapter 26
Life In and Out of the High Desert

We decide to sell the Las Vegas house and move all our furniture to the small place in Arizona.

Twan, David and Dalys are living in Arizona. Connie and Bash live in Mesa, Arizona. Jerome and Michael live in California. He is in the United States Marine Corps!

Turning the high desert mobile home from a get-a-way, to full time residence means a lot of work, and not only repairs, we also need more room. We remodel and add a hot tub and gazebo, a carport (to support our three vehicles), and everything else to make life comfortable.

"This is probably the nicest furnished mobile home in Arizona!" Mother said.

Being a recluse, Ron loves the high desert.

"Merry Christmas," I tell Ron and introduce him to Cleo, a Pekingese. As long as the dog is near, Ron is happy.

Sam and Judy Maney live a mile down the road and are our closest neighbors. We grow to love them.

Living in the desert gives you the feeling of being on your own and secure, because no matter what happens anywhere else in the world, it has little effect on day-to-day life in the desert.

The turn of the century found everyone very curious as to what would happen when the clock struck midnight and the year 2000 would arrive! Computers seem to be running everything and the warning even reaches us in the desert.

"All the computers are configured to the 20th Century (1900 to 1999). When 2000 comes, will all the computers crash?"

Nobody knows what was going to happen. Will the banks lose their data? Will stores close down? Will the government shut down? What about the mail? Fear of the unknown leads many to take extra precautions.

People buy extra food and water. Survival kits are sold. Many buy property in locations far away from cities. Toilet paper is a prized commodity.

I am 55 years old. Ron and I are among the skeptics. We live in the perfect location. We even convert the greater part of our savings into numismatic coins, gold, silver, and platinum coins, as well as bulk silver. Since we do not know if the banks will survive, we bury this "stash" underground in the carport of our mobile home.

"Why don't you all come to see the New Year in with us?" I invite Mother, Twan and her children along with Connie and Bash to our secluded corner of the world. Ron and the kids went to bed early and slept the entire evening. We ladies stayed awake and when the year 2000 arrived, we are playing an X-rated game! I will not give the details of that game, but if you want to know what it was, feel free to ask any one of us at your convenience. Shameful! We should have never played such a game!!!

As hindsight speaks, all the worry was unnecessary. For us, Y2K came and went with little incident and we had a six months' supply of toilet paper.

I like the high desert, but solitude has its limits. I am not one who loves being alone. I start going on trips and stay away, more than I am at home. Ron is content and has no problem with my being gone. I spend time at Mother's, Twan's, Connie's, friends in California, etc. It does not seem to be a problem, being gone so much.

The 21st Century does not start well for my sister. In June, Perry Jo is again a widow, facing life as a single parent with a child in junior high. Her third husband, Ray Jones, dies suddenly and unexpected.

Two months later, we receive another devastating call from my niece, Marlee.

"Aunt Suzie, DeDe is dead," she says with tears in her voice. DeDe is Perry's oldest daughter. The silence, after her words, tells me she is serious.

"That seems impossible!" is all I can reply.

We had recently made an emergency trip to Texas, and saw the agony and heartache of their loss. We experienced the sorrow of watching my sister grieve. I could not imagine Perry being hit with this news of her daughter's death, particularly this soon after the loss of her husband.

"We had a huge July 4th celebration with food and fireworks," said Marlee. This year Perry's son, Jeff, hosted the event in their new country house. DeDe not only went to this party but she traveled back and forth down the little country roads to her in-laws, for their celebration as well. Around midnight, between the two homes, DeDe, while driving alone, lost control of her car and hit a tree. She died immediately. *My brother later wrote a story about it in his book, Inquest: Living With the Dead.*

Ron and I sadly pack our bags and head back to Texas.

I realize I may be wearing out my welcome, visiting the different places I take refuge, so Ron and I buy an older house located half way between Mother's house and

Perry's. The Bolton House is about a half mile from each. We take some of our "stuff" there and make it a comfortable second home. I now realize the importance of being near family and we began dividing our time between Arizona and Texas. Life is good.

From Winona, I occasionally make the 538-mile trip south to Harlingen, Texas, to see Jerome and Michelle. Jerome is now in the Border Patrol. On June 29, 2001, we receive Paul Jacob Murphy into the family! Yes, my third grandchild/second grandson was born. What a blessing he is and continues to be a wonderful addition to our family.

Connie and Bash are doing well! She meets Brad Lober and a love story is set into motion! Brad moves into Connie's house and takes the role of dad to Sebastian. Before long, August 16, 2002 to be exact, Benjamin Cole Lober was born! Ben is my third grandson/fifth grandchild! What another blessing! I claim the "Cole" in his name as being my namesake!

On February 1, 2003, Connie and Brad get married in Sedona, Arizona. I help plan their lovely wedding. We have a large reception at their home in Scottsdale and everything goes amazingly well.

In May, we decide to try the "Motorhome" lifestyle. After all, we like to travel and why not live like a turtle and carry our mobile house around with us. We can go wherever we want, stop wherever we want, sleep whenever we want. Ron and I get a great deal on a used motor home. Almost everything works, except the toilet, which should not be a problem; after all, we will be on the road! Our first trip will be taking a long scenic route to Texas.

Cleo, the Pekingese, has puppies that are six weeks

old. We plan to stop at Connie's in Scottsdale and sell them.

"I have nausea and diarrhea," I tell Ron. For the past few years, I have been diagnosed as obese. During these "fat" years, I have dealt with high blood pressure, sugar diabetes, and glaucoma. None of these have given me an incentive to lose weight.

Seldom having ever been sick, I continue our plans, thinking that any minute I will feel fine again.

"Let's go," insists Ron.

"I am still sick. I guess I can be sick at home or on the road." We leave on schedule.

In Scottsdale, we advertise the six puppies and sell five of them the next day. There is one runt, which nobody wants. She is a keeper and Cleo is now a proud mother. Buffy, at seven weeks old, is our new traveling companion in the "Motorhome Express."

The Accident
Part 5
Cleo R.I.P.

It is hard to believe that less than twenty-four hours ago, Ron and Elizabeth, with their pups, made the cold early morning exit from East Texas. Everything is suddenly put on hold. Elizabeth's loved ones drop everything to travel to Midland, to wait and pray.

After surgery, the surgeon, Dr. Sawyer, informs the family, "Elizabeth's small intestines were injured, actually squashed during the accident. One foot of the small bowel had to be removed and the remaining was successfully repaired. It is now a wait-and-see situation."

"Will she be OK?"

"Looking toward the future," says Dr. Sawyer, "she can live without that one foot of intestines. Her lifestyle will need to be modified but she can live with it."

With that news, everyone is relieved, with a renewed sense of hope. Positive attitudes and prayers with confidence are offered! What a welcomed breath of fresh air!

Sunday morning Elizabeth awakes in the hospital room and starts to grasp the extent of yesterday's events! A large tube is down her throat, which makes it impossible for her to speak. In her frail manner, she can only communicate by writing on a drawing board. Other tubes and all sorts of paraphernalia are extending from her body.

She sees a great host of friends and family coming into her room two by two. They are smiling and yet, their eyes show an expression of great sympathy. These souls are medicine to Elizabeth's body. Feeling the love serves as a healing ointment for her body! Even her dear friend, Jeann, has flown in from Washington D.C.

"I thought she was dead! I went to the other room where she was, but she wasn't there. I thought she died!" Elizabeth saw Jeann embracing Lolo and it snapped into her mind, as if a photo.

Elizabeth sees Ron. It is the first time she is aware enough to know he is in the room. As he approaches, it is clear he is very distressed. He bends over Elizabeth. She expects words of consolation, pity, maybe even, "I'm sorry." With tears and intense passion, Ron blurts out, "Cleo didn't make it!"

A little confused Elizabeth looks for her drawing board. "Cleo didn't make it?" she wants to say. "What's that all about?" The tablet is not on her bed table and she struggles to set up and look for it. She can only say to herself, "I am laying here barely alive, only to hear Cleo died?" She reaches over and pats the top of the nightstand without success, looking for the tablet. She thought, "Very sorry, but this is not a time that I want to comprehend such news." Then she sees Ron as a grieving parent and wants to express sympathy, but she only closes her eyes in sadness.

Cleo and Buffy were a team and they were protected and loved by both Ron and Elizabeth. It was understood that Cleo belonged to Ron. Buffy never seemed to mature and always acted like a baby, so she was considered Elizabeth's dog.

Day 2: Christians are a peculiar people, especially the Christians in Elizabeth's family. They not only love and revere God, but they trust and realize that He has complete control of their lives.

Elizabeth's brother, Mitch, drives to Midland, bringing Leola. She is gravely shaken and quickly at the bedside of her daughter.

During one's lifetime, a person is very fortunate if they come into contact and get to know a lady such as Leola. She is one of those people who is a magnet to everyone. Being a Godly woman, she is loved. Her conversation is usually uplifting with words of wisdom and a bit of knowledge about everything!

Ron is bruised, stiff and very sore from the impact of yesterday's accident. Sadness of Cleo's death and bestowing the bulk of his loving care on Buffy, he remains, to a large degree, alone. "There is nothing much for me to do," he tells Elizabeth. "You are getting all the attention you need. Everyone you know has come here to dote over you!"

The hospital staff realizes this clan is a different brew! They develop a particular liking to this caring and close knit Christian family! There is so much love, such compassion and at the same time, there is strength, which creates a carefree and confident atmosphere.

On lookers in the hospital waiting room are amazed watching the family. They are cheerful; they have good confessions with positive dispositions, declaring however, this turns out, "Our God reigns." Gail Wilson, the hospital chaplain, stays close to the side of everyone with her uplifting confirmation that God's will is being done.

Gale is invaluable as she reinforced the ways of God to the family. Marlee drew close to Gale as their Spirits united as one! *They have a special bond to this day. It is amazing how certain events can create lasting friendship*

Gale composes the following prayer to God, and to

give the family strength.

Father,

   I come to you on behalf of my dear sister-in-Christ and I KNOW that you are present in the midst of this great trial in her life and I praise you because you have shown yourself to be Devine in her life. Elizabeth loves you with her whole heart and presents herself as a Proverbs 31:10-30 woman. I think you for her witness.

   Father, I ask that your angels of ministry surround her family and friends. May they feel and know the supernatural peace that only comes from you. Give them your wisdom and discernment, give them eyes to see, give them ears to hear you. May their lives be guided by your perfect will at this moment and in the days ahead.

   Father, I rebuke this infection in Elizabeth's body; I ask that you heal her body in a supernatural way that she may be healed and restored to normal function and I command her immune system to work properly and all of her systems begin to work in harmony with each other. I rebuke any unclean vessels that are coming against Elizabeth and I rebuke them in Jesus' name.

   Father, go ahead of the surgical staff, guide the hands, eyes and hearts of all who will be involved in the care of Elizabeth and her surgery tomorrow morning. I pray for rested bodies and alert minds as well as strong convictions with a sense of knowing that you are God. Should someone involved in her case not know you as Lord and Savior, may they come to know you during this process and may you be glorified.

I thank you for allowing me to come into your throne on behalf of Elizabeth; I humbly submit her to you and release her into your arms and thank you for she is safe in your arms.

In the most powerful name in all creation, Jesus Christ, I pray this. Amen and Amen

Peace...Be still.
Gale Wilson

Call to me and I will answer you and tell you great and unsearchable things you do not know. Jeremiah 33:3 (NIV)

"It is as if they know a secret," says the clerk at the nurse's desk. "They have a special peace and calmness during this storm."

Who does not live in peace when their confidence is in God?

He will keep in perfect peace him whose mind is steadfast, because he trusts in God.

Isaiah 26:3

Sister Perry is among those waiting at the hospital. After one of her frequent cigarette breaks, she enters the waiting room. Her deep voice catches everyone's attention as she proclaims, "I am positive my sister will come through this. I have had two husbands who died sudden deaths, and a daughter killed in a wreck. I know God would never allow my sister to be tragically taken away from me too. Besides, she cannot die. Too many people would lose their only friend! A lot of people depend on her friendship. Believe me, she won't die." After a short hesitation Perry sternly adds, "She will be just fine; she will recover one hundred percent. I'm confident of this. Do not pray that she will just live and get better. Pray for one hundred percent recovery and nothing less!"

Everyone had been at Lolo's birthday only days before. Now they are sharing love as if they had not seen each other for years. The demeanor changes from a solemn time of concern, to jokes and fun.

"Jerome, it has been so long!" Connie jokes as she and Twan rush to give their brother a hug. Only last week, they had flown from different directions into Dallas and rented a car to attend the surprise birthday party! That celebration was a special time for them and the first time ever being together as adults, just the three siblings without spouses and children.

"Jewelry, Bible, van" Elizabeth wrote on her drawing pad. It was not easy, but she was able to get across to the kids she didn't want to lose those things to a wreck!

Twan and Connie decide to make a run to the crash site and the wrecked vehicle. Borrowing a car, off they go.

"This is eerie," says Twan, shivering from the cold. They look around the silent wrecking yard. "It's a graveyard for cars. This place looks like a bomb has been dropped."

"Where is the van?" asks Connie. They wander around, looking at all the other vehicles involved in multiple pile-ups.

"There it is. The van is still on the wrecker!" Twan motions and they hasten their pace. First, they notice the passenger door, forced ajar by the medics. Still open it is pressed against the front fender. They climb upon the wrecker and walk around the edge of the flatbed.

"Here's Mom's cell phone," exclaims Connie. "But, over there is the cross charm attachment for it. How did all this stuff get so scattered around?" Connie could not believe the mess. "Mom loaded up on this trip!" As they salvage around the van, they begin to throw things to the ground. Luggage, odds and ends, "This is stuff that only Mom would want."

"How could she have filled the van this full?" asks Twan pulling out a plastic bubble wrapped crushed stained glass window. "It's shattered to smithereens."

"How did that chair get wedged between the front seats?" And here is the Bible in the floorboard." Many things had no sentimental value, but at the same time, many things did.

"Can you imagine this?" Twan asks as she lifts up the Waterford crystal vase. "Not a scratch!"

They suddenly stop.

"Oh no!" Twan sighs. Their eyes target the sight at precisely the same second. It is not a pretty picture. Cleo is still in the crumpled van.

Cleo is curdled up in a hard ball. Buried against the back seat and lying amid the debris; her furry body is icy and rigid.

"Ron said the man in the wrecker would handle Cleo. If this is his idea of a joke, it is not a good one," says Connie

"Hello! Over here." They wave at someone in the salvage yard. He is wearing greasy overalls so they hope he works there.

"Cleo is still in the car!" He looks confused.

"She is dead!" He looks very confused.

"The dog, Cleo, is still in the van."

"Oh, da dog," is his response. "You can have it too," He looks around at all the stuff, most of it broken, scattered on the ground.

"Would you help us bury her? The wrecker driver said he was going to take care of her."

"Can't burry 'er here. And I aren't the wrecker driver," he walks away.

"WE have to bury Cleo."

The last two things they load into the borrowed car is Cleo's bed with Cleo in it. They close the trunk lid. Cleo's cold and stiff body is in the trunk with all of the other, mostly broken, possessions.

Now what? They agree this is a moment-by-moment decision-making time.

"I have a cyber-friend in Midland. Maybe she has a shovel," Connie mummers while still thinking.

Connie tries to make contact, but to no avail. Getting flustered, the two begin to take drastic measures!

"Stop here!" One of them shouts, "Let's put Cleo over on the other side of that fence! I think for now it's the best we can do."

They stop, get out and retrieve Cleo's stiff body. She is not the cute fluffy dog they had known. Now her body is ghastly. Whatever sign of life she had yesterday disappeared with wetness, ice and rigor mortis.

"Surely we can get her over the fence." They walk and the terrain gets rough and the weeds get deeper.

"Do rattlesnakes get out in this weather?" Connie asks.

The closer they get to the fence the taller it is.

After much trying, Twan and Connie are getting nervous and frustrated. They want to do the right thing, but there are too many complications. Besides, "Our mother is in the hospital, possibly dying! Let's try to gently throw Cleo over the fence. We've got to end this!"

That is just what they did.

Connie and Twan have had many "out of the ordinary" experiences during their lifetimes, but none quite like this.

"Goodbye Cleo!" they yell and wave as they get in the car, then they burst out laughing and start to relax.

"Heck of a day!" says Connie.

"I'm glad it is over," replies Twan. "We should have buried her but she is gone to Doggie Heaven. It is just her cold dead body lying there."

"You think something will eat her. Like a buzzard or coyote or something?"

"Maybe or maybe someone will find her."

"Oh No! She still has her collar and tags on." The car stops.

"We can't leave her with her identification. Someone will find her and call Ron!" They panic. "We can't just leave her out there like that. We have to go back, get her and bury her properly." Connie insists. Off they go to get Cleo, again.

"There she is," exclaims Connie. "Just as we left her: wet, cold, stiff and now dirty. It's cold and getting colder."

"So go get her," Twan urges.

"No! It was your idea to throw her over the fence."

"Are you sure?"

"And you are so much better at climbing fences than I am." Connie adds. "How about you just get the tags?"

After some choice words, Twan climbs the fence and hops down on the other side. While Twan is removing the tags, Connie yells, "This is not where Cleo's remains should be."

Cleo ungracefully flies back over the fence. She is carried across the Midland Desert and put back into the trunk of the car.

"I'm starving," says Twan. It is way past time to eat and they are ravenous.

They drive into a Sonic drive-in.

Their order is repeated over the speaker. "That will be large lemonade, a large Pepsi and two foot long chili-cheese dogs. Would you like fries with that?"

"That's all," and they wait for their meal to come.

"This has been entirely too much!" confesses Connie.

"Mother might be dying and here we are spending all day with a dead dog. This is not right!"

"That will be $8.75," said the bundled up server.

"Here and keep the change."

"Sick. We're eating hot dogs while Cleo is still in the trunk! I think I smell her."

"Did you wash your hands?" The appetites disappear and the hot dogs go into the Sonic trash: "Guess we don't need a doggie bag!" Connie laughs as they drive into the sunset.

Now desperate and exhausted, they turn off the main road onto an old black top road. The area looks peaceful and secluded. A few miles down the oil road, they turn off on a dirt road.

"This reminds me of the old days and parking in the oil fields." They pull up beside an oilrig. Maybe it is still in use, but it is quiet and no one is around.

Twan and Connie stop and get out of the car. With much relief they agree, "This is the perfect spot." It is a Utopia, peaceful and quiet. Certainly, this is the best resting place for Cleo. Like pallbearers, they reverently carry the doggie bed like a casket and set it on the ground. Solemnly and with few words, the two are off again.

Shivering from the cold, they return to the car. Connie never looks back, but Twan does. She sees Cleo lying peacefully and a light breeze ruffles through her hair.

"Cleo, rest in peace."

Chapter 27
Rapid Weight Loss Diet (Not recommended)

Ron, Buffy, Cleo and sick me leave Connie's on the third day in our motor home destined for Texas. The unlimited carefree trip we dreamed of was not to be. My sickness gets worse and worse. My nausea escalates to vomiting and the diarrhea intensifies and liquefies! As Ron drives the highways of Arizona, New Mexico and forever across Texas, I am standing in the RV, regurgitating in a bag while at the same time holding another bag to my rear and having diarrhea. I cannot control either. I have never been this sick in my life.

"Drive on and buy gas," are my instructions to Ron. "I can't eat! I can't even get out of the motor home." I am rapidly going downhill.

It takes several days, which seem like months, to arrive in East Texas.

"Meet us at Medical Center Emergency Room. Suzie's sick." Ron tells the family. Perry arrives as Ron is checking me in.

"I need help. I can't sit still. I am so sick."

"The Doctor will be in shortly," says the nurse.

"I need help. I can't lie down." I am squirming from one chair to another.

"The Doctor will be in shortly," says another nurse.

"I need help!" I am pacing around the room.

"The Doctor will be in shortly," repeats still another nurse.

"I need help!" I roam from seat to seat when I am not running back and forth to the bathroom, vomiting every few minutes.

"I can't find a nurse" says Perry. It has been well over an hour.

"Please take me somewhere else."

We go to the University of Texas Research Center/Hospital near Winona. After some time, I finally see a doctor. They give me a quart of IV fluid and tell me to return in the morning.

The next morning early, I am sitting in the doctor's treatment room.

"You weigh 152 pounds," says Doctor Zembeah.

"Two weeks ago I weighed 162," I reply, as the doctor continues to look, listen, and poke me.

"You are very sick," announces the Doctor. That proves to me that he learned something in his eight years of medical school in whatever country he is from.

"We shall admit you to the hospital." And the tests begin. Test, one after another, and they do not find anything wrong. A new diagnosis is "gastro paresis" which is a type of paralyses of the digestive system.

"Reglan is a new drug made just for this disorder," prescribes the Doctor. "It is important that you take one thirty minutes before each meal."

They try several different medications that seem to work. I go home one day only to go back the next just as sick as before.

For over a month it is more hospital for more tests. Nothing I eat will stay down, yet I am continually dirtying the diapers I now have to wear. My weight continues to drop. I look pathetic; every family member is very concerned. It seems as though I am dying before their eyes. My cousin Lane drives up from Rockport, Texas, to try and help save me. Several old friends, whom I have not seen in years, come by to visit me. (Kathy Dale, Jenny & Chester in particular) It is as though everyone is telling me goodbye. Nobody knows what to do.

My niece, Lena, is having her wedding at the

Winona Methodist Church, June 15, 2003.

"Of course you're going! Suzie, it's just downtown! Your brother's wedding ceremonies aren't long," Perry continues. "I've got just the dress for you! You've lost so much weight. I bet you can wear DeDe's clothes. I've been saving this dress for something special, and it looks like this is that special time." She holds up an exquisite black silk dress with beads and sequins!

The dress fits perfectly and I attend a beautiful wedding. I try to stay for the reception but I only last a few minutes when weakness and nausea overtake me.

"I think Ron is trying to poison you," alleges a concerned family member. "Think about it. You check into the hospital and get better only to go home and get sick again."

At 115 pounds, I am not only thin; I cannot stand or walk without help. I cry continually, make strange facial expressions, have cramps and muscle spasms. When I sit or lay down my legs are jumping up and down with an extreme case of RLS. (Restless Leg Syndrome)

"We have to do something else. Trying the same thing over and over is crazy," demands Mother.

"You are wasting away, dying before our eyes," my kids join in.

"The Mayo Clinic is famous for its gastroenterology department," says Connie, who accepts the challenge.

The Winona family puts me on a plane to Arizona bound for the Mayo Clinic in Scottsdale, Arizona.

Connie and Brad receive me with open arms. Both she and Brad do everything in their power to make me comfortable.

Getting into the Mayo Clinic is no easy task. Connie has to connect me with a primary care physician, who must refer me to the Mayo Clinic. At this point, I can do nothing for myself. I am acting crazy, continually whining, constantly rocking back and forth with nonstop leg movements. Connie tries to force me to eat. This ends with me shouting, crying, vomiting everywhere and making a mess. I still have to wear diapers at all times.

My first doctor visit is on a Friday with Dr. Marks.

"Are you a Christian?" I ask.

"No!" is his reply. In my condition, why did I even ask?

"Here are my medical records from Texas." I hand him three manila folders 3 inches thick. There are volumes of test results with notes from the many hospital tests and doctor visits I had during the past couple of months.

Dr. Marks is stunned, "I want to take all these records home and study them over the weekend. I want you back here Monday morning,"

Monday morning Connie and I are in the doctor's office.

"These medical records are impeccable!" said Dr. Marks. "I am in full agreement with the UT Health Center's conclusions. Everything seems normal, but you are sick." Great, we have another medical school success story.

"So why am I so sick and what is wrong with me?"

Dr. Marks suggest I continue taking daily handfuls of prescribed medicine and make appointments with different specialists.

"Here is a list of specialists," he says handing Connie two pages of names and addresses. "By seeing each different specialist, one will finally stumble upon your problem."

"If she lives long enough!" declares Connie.

Appointments with the more specialists produce nothing. Connie is determined to solve the mystery. In three months, I have gone from 162 pounds to 106 and I appear to be a gibbering idiot!

Another appointment another gastroenterologist (GI doctor), I am in no condition to plea my own case. The doctor listens as Connie tells him my symptoms.

"What test did they do to diagnose of gastro paresis?" He immediately orders me to cease the drug Reglan. "I do not think you have gastro paresis at all."

I am being poisoned, by a doctor! I took a Reglan pill thirty minutes before every meal, for the last three months! The whole ordeal started with a stomach disorder. I am now experiencing the bad side effects of Reglan. I could have died, and almost did, before we discover the solution!

I start my recovery weighing 99 pounds. I cannot bring myself to eat again. The trauma of eating during the last three mounts has ruined my appetite.

"We can put in a feeding tube and get some meat back on your bones," says Dr. Marks.

"No way!" is my reply. I can only think of old people dying with a feeding tube keeping them alive. I am not ready to die.

It takes a psychologist to get my mind straight and start eating again. The Restless Legg Syndrome, the Tardive Dyskinesia (unusual muscle movements) and distorted facial expressions ceased after a few weeks of being off the drug Reglan.

In 2010, seven years later, an extensive study was released about Reglan and its devastating side effects. There was a large lawsuit brought against them by patients previously affected by the drug. Usually those dreadful side effects, experienced by people allergic to the drug, are permanent. My side effects reversed, which I view as another miracle in the life of Suzie.

I am eternally thankful to Dr. Marks (who, by the way, is Jewish) for steering us in the right direction. Forever I shall acknowledge Connie and Brad for being patient and putting up with this crazy lady until she regained her wits.

This illness consumed six months of my life. My weight now stays between 108 and 113 pounds! After a full recovery and the weight loss, doctors took me off medications for sugar diabetes, high blood pressure and glaucoma!
I lost 63 pounds in three months! Not the way anyone would chose to lose it, but God took the bad and worked it for my good! I praise God for this.

This is indeed a **RAPID WEIGHT LOSS DIET**, but I do not recommend it to anyone

I gradually regain my health and strength and continue to have weekly doctor appointments. My kids do not place much confidence in Ron's ability to care for me, so Twan suggests I stay in Scottsdale with Clare.
Clare Ehrmann is a friend of a friend of a friend, whom I have crossed paths with a few times. Twan calls and tells her of our situation.
"It is a four hour drive from the high desert, every week, to see the doctor. If Mom can stay with you it will be wonderful."
"Of course!" declares Clare. "I would love to have

the company. I've got a guest room and she is welcome to it."

Clare is quite a character. She starts her morning with beer for breakfast. Every day she has the same routine of beer until noon. Then it is Vodka and tonic water for the rest of the day. Her health is great and her sense of humor matches mine.

"Thank you for putting up with me for these past few weeks" I tell Clare. "I have no more doctor appointments and I am back on my feet. I don't have any excuses to stay around."

"You don't need any excuse to stay here," says Clare. "My guestroom is always open to you." And with that, it is back to Ron and the high desert. However, not for long.

"I have been cooped up long enough," I began my habit of wandering. I spend very little time at the high desert home.

"Ron, why don't you buy a house in Scottsdale?" questions Connie.

"We have a house in Winona and the high desert home. We can't afford another vacation house," Ron explains.

"If I can find you a place for less than $20,000, would you buy it?" Connie lays out the challenge.

Ron jokingly answers, "If you can find one at that price I'll eat it!"

Within two hours, Connie has an appointment for us to look at a one-bedroom unit in South Scottsdale.

"Ok, we'll buy it!" It is a small apartment in the Aberdeen Co-Ops subdivision. Within two days, we seal the deal.

We intend it to be our escape in Scottsdale: for Ron

or me or both of us.

We have another place! We both enjoy the excitement of putting another house together and decorating. We plan to take some of our high desert furniture to Scottsdale and set it up as another residence for us.

"Nita needs me in California," I tell Ron. "She is sick and I am committing to help her for at least a week or more."

Therefore, Ron drives north to the high desert and I fly west to California.

Chapter 28
Fire In The High Desert

I had been in California for several days when I received a phone call from Ron. He was excited and talking fast.

I interrupted, "Ron, slow down, I can't understand what you're saying," After a few more incoherent words, he finally calmed down.

He slowly said, "I'm watching our trailer burn to the ground! Cleo and Buffy were on the back deck, they are OK."

Still excited he told me the story. The mobile home caught on fire while he was outside.

"It is burning so fast there is no way to save anything," he shouts. "I had the cell phone in my pocket and that is how we are talking. The fire is still raging, everything is lost."

My mind was going crazy with questions and I even gave a list of instructions.

"It is almost to the carport now!" he stated in desperation.

"There is a car key under the back bumper!" I yell into the phone. "Get what you can out of the carport," and I realize there is no one on the other end of the line.

"We saved the Grand-Am but the Corvette is gone." The extra protection of the custom cover was between him and his classic Corvette. He was forced to watch the fiberglass body melt to the ground and his muscle car burn into a twisted clump of metal. Other than his dogs, the Corvette was his most prized possession.

Ron called Sam and Judy Maney, who were our

good friends and had moved to Kingman (70 miles away). Sam drove to the high desert and stayed with Ron until the fire department left.

After everyone had gone, Ron confided in Sam. "There is something we need to get." They located a tool to dig with and dug until they found the thick hot plastic bag loaded with gold and silver. This bag Ron had buried over three years ago! Ron did not look inside; he simply took it with him to Sam's house.

Material things meant a lot to Ron. All of his gold jewelry was on the bar in the kitchen. That was now gone. All of his clothes, literally everything on the property had turned to ashes.

The following day, Ron picked me up in Vegas driving the Grand-Am. Thank God, I told him about the key before it was too late. We met with the insurance agent while in Las Vegas. I had not yet seen the devastation but I envisioned being able to recover at least some of our things.

I was shocked! There was a blackened heap of rubble and nothing left to search through. The local volunteer fire department took thirty minutes getting there, so all they could do was to contain the fire and water the ashes. They demolished everything with heavy equipment to make sure the fire was dead.

"It is useless spending any time looking here because there isn't anything left." Late in the evening, we returned to Vegas and I flew back to Nita's.

Twan lived in California so I went there after I completed my Nita obligation. The following weekend, we drove to Meadview to review the mess.

"There has to be something here," I said. Twan,

Dalys, Alyssa and I rambled through the debris. Among the ruins were numerous copper and brass pots, pans, and vases, which Ron had bought while living in Iran.

"These are hand tooled and valuable antiques." I pointed out. "There has to be something of value left."

I found a wheelbarrow and estimated where the kitchen bar would have been. I got a shovel and started shoveling ashes. Each time the wheelbarrow was full; I would take it afar and sift through the ashes one handful at a time. I spent several hours doing this.

"Here is Ron's college graduation ring with the emerald cut diamond in it." I found another gold ring and neither were melted. "They'll clean up and be as good as new!"

"What about the gold watch?" asked Dalys, holding up the damaged timepiece? *I later had a jeweler turn the watch into a sigma ring for Ron. The top of the ring has the watch imprint that was once the back of the watch. It is unique and he often received compliments on it.*

As for my loss? The Winona house was partially furnished and there were a few clothes there. Most of my favorite clothes are with me. As for my jewelry, I usually carried the bulk of it with me, so most of it did not burn.

The loss for Ron was devastating. He lost his Corvette. I had dropped the insurance, with his approval. It was seldom driven. Ron insisted we keep it covered in the carport and refused to put miles on it. The 1984 Corvette, now twenty-one years old, had less than 65,000 miles. We had recently bought a new set of tires.

Ron originally stated that he was outside working in the yard when he noticed the fire. Later, after interrogation, he confessed that he was burning trash in our illegal burn barrel. Burning debris fell out of the barrel causing the mobile home to go up in flames.

Over the years an item, dress, jewelry, vase, a document or a thing will come to mind and I wonder what happened to it. After a concentrated effort to remember, I realize it turned to ashes in the fire of our past.

Another aspect to the "fire story" is a wonderful example of God's provision.

Throughout my lifetime, I have been blessed to watch God in action as my life unfolds. Remember the co-op we purchased just days before in Scottsdale? The timing was perfect. We spent one month in a hotel while having it remodeled. The fire insurance paid quickly and there were no complaints concerning that.

I marvel at the work of God! I enjoy His daily activity with me. Most of all I enjoy God's great love for me. It is available to everyone, but not everyone has that knowledge. The only requirement to receive God's attention is to seek it, look for Him in each and every aspect of your life. Read His word and get to know God's personality. Intentionally, seek God with all your heart and you will find Him. He has already found you! How simple is that?

From 2003 until 2008, our home base was the Aberdeen Cooperative units in Scottsdale. We sold the one bedroom unit and bought a larger one. We were both members of the Board of Directors. Ron was president for several years. We still owned the older home in Winona and spent time there. We loved our two Pekingese puppies, Cleo and Buffy. Ron and I were happy enough. We took several cruises, went to Vegas and Laughlin to do a little gambling and I made several trips a year to Texas to visit family and manage the rental properties.

Chapter 29
Good Years In Scottsdale

"What shall we name the baby?" Jerome and Michelle and Connie and Brad are both having babies. They are pregnant at the same time and both carrying girls.

My mother, Evie Leola Shamburger, is the matriarch of our family. She has been a major influence on my children. She is the appeals process when my kids disagree with me. Michelle and Connie comment that there should never be a time when LoLo is forgotten. After consideration, both families decide to honor Evie Leola Shamburger with a namesake.

On August 15, 2005, Evie Star Murphy is born! Evie is my sixth grandchild/third granddaughter.

On November 8, 2005, Leola Helene Lober arrives! Leola is my seventh grandchild/fourth granddaughter. God has truly blessed!

Ron and I are active in our community and continue to be on the board of our co-op. I have grown close to all the Miller family in Arizona: Sally and Ryan, Mimi and Ray with their kids and Judy, Troy and Tad. The Millers are actually Marv's family, but they treat me, like Perry, as family! I am introduced as, "Sister-in-law"; and their children call me "Aunt Tuzie!" What a blessing!

In June, 2007 Connie and Brad move to California to be near Twan and her family. This leaves Ron and me in Scottsdale, which is fine with us. We have many friends, a church we love and of course, we think of the Millers as family. Jerome and Michelle are living in Sierra Vista, which is a short three-hour drive south.

The Accident
Part 6
A Trip through Hell

Have all these people rushed to Midland only to leave Elizabeth alone? Once they see she is not going to die, is it time to quit? Is an adrenalin flow and the excitement of someone dying all there is? Does life go back to normal for everyone but Elizabeth?

"Back to normal" is a vast understatement. This troop of soldiers is not of this world! They are in God's army. As the Bible says, "We fight not against flesh and blood, but against rulers, against the powers of this dark world and against the spiritual forces of evil in the heavenly realms." Ephesians 6:12. Normal, for these warriors, is daily bringing Light into the world through prayer and causing change for the good of others, by living a life pleasing to God.

Elizabeth is not alone. They are leaving in body only! Through prayer and their consciousness of life through the Spirit of God, they remain with her. We are one in the Spirit; we are one in the Lord. Elizabeth is not alone at all!

In addition, Perry and her mother remain in town to support and to aid in Elizabeth's recovery.

Elizabeth is experiencing excruciating pain all the time. With her mother and sister at the hospital, she would be distracted during the daytime.

Perry is a great cheerleader. She spends hours forcing Elizabeth to suck up the pain and to obey the hospital staff. Elizabeth cries during the rehabilitation sessions. It hurts her to stand and it is especially painful to try to take steps. Perry often says, "No pain no gain."

When Lolo and Perry return to their hotel in the evenings, it is a different story. The nights seem endless! The pain surmounts to the point that Elizabeth does not want to survive!

She is not a good patient. "I can handle almost anything life hands me, just don't give me pain!" she would say. Well, now she had no choice but to endure the pain and battle infections.

No appetite, constant pain, constant diarrhea - life is intolerable.

"If this is progress I'll be dead when I'm well," Elizabeth tells the doctor.

"You are ready to go," announces Doctor Sawyer. It has been two weeks since the accident. "Elizabeth is strong enough to complete the trip to a rehabilitation facility in Arizona! We have made all the arrangements."

On March 1, 6:00 pm Elizabeth waves goodbye to her mother and sister. She watches them shrink away through the ambulance back window. They swoosh away from Midland for a **trip through Hell.**

Twelve endless hours, I am riding on my back in the dark of the night. The ambulance is cold with no shock absorbers. Every bump is magnified ten times and feels like a knife, jabbing into my belly. Running over those plastic reflective "dots" in the middle of the road feels like being shot with a machine gun.

"They are killing me," I cry to Marlee on my cell phone.

"You're going to be OK," she tries to sooth me. "When you get to the hospital it will get better."

"If I make it! Scottsdale is ten more hours away and I don't think I will last that long. I am hurting. I don't know if I want to last that long."

"Hang in there," she says. Cheerleading like her mother. "Relax, and do what they tell you. See if you can get something..." the cell phone is dead. Maybe I am next!

"Please, I'm begging you. Stop and do something." The two medics look at each other. It is all they can do. "Here it comes again." I tell them as a warning. As bad as it sounds, the fact is, my bowels are uncontrollable. I cannot control or manage myself, nor can I stop crying. The ambulance crew stops twice, only to refuel and get back on the road. Even with my constant prayers, I think the night will never end!

As the early morning dawn breaks, the ambulance drives into Scottsdale. Very weak and tired, I have to direct the driver to our destination. The attendants were curious.

"How do you know when we need to turn and what exits we are at?" ask one of the medics.

"I'm magic!" I answer. "And I am thinking about putting a curse on you two for not stopping when I wanted you to." Actually, the direction in which I am lying gives me privy to the large mirrors stationed outside, toward the rear of the ambulance. I can see in the mirrors and, although the words are backwards, I can read the upcoming exit signs. I know where the rehabilitation facility is.

I call Ron to finalize the arrangements. "Ron we are in town and on the way to the rehab facility. They know when we should arrive and a room will be ready. Bring my Bible and I will see you when I get there."

Ron was not there, nor was the room ready!

"All I want is to be cleaned up and put in a bed." I declare this to the ambulance guys. It has been thirty minutes and they are the only ones who are standing by.

"Mrs. Colman, we can't seem to find your records," The limited night crew is rushing about.

"Try Cole, C O L E." There is havoc everywhere.

"We have a temporary room," says someone holding a clipboard.

They wheel the gurney into a room that does not have a hospital bed. There is a couch and a bathroom.

Not realizing my delicate condition, they are less than gentle. They lift me off the gurney, "Oops!" they drop me! The two attendants look at each other and quickly pick me up and place me on the couch. This did not add to my pain, it did add to my frustration!

The attendants run out of the room before I can tell them what I think of their patient care abilities.

I call my sister crying, "It was a ride from Hell. They are not ready for me. Nobody seems to know anything. Ron isn't here, and to top it all off, they dropped me!"

Finally, Ron arrives. Eventually, I am wheel chaired to my real room and cleaned up! I am exhausted. I care about nothing else! Just let me sleep.

I wake up on day three and I am still not over that awful ambulance ride.

Chapter 30
The Buried Treasure

I enjoy my many trips back to Texas. Even cleaning up a rental house after someone has absconded with my rent money works out fine for me. Sometimes cleaning means just that: sweeping, moping and scrubbing. Other times it means a complete makeover: painting, flooring, even plumbing and electrical work.

I hire out the heavy work, roll up my sleeves and do what I can to save money and get the house ready for the next tenant. I am scrubbing sinks in the kitchen when I hear someone at the open front door.

"Hello." I recognize the voice of Jeff Miller, my nephew.

"Come on in."

"Are you working? I came by to visit but I don't want to interrupt you."

"Perfect timing, I am tired. You want a Dr. Pepper?" We sit down for a chat. "It's been a while."

"Yes it has. You know family should get together more often," says Jeff. If someone is missing at a family gathering, it is usually Jeff. Jeff likes to talk, and thinks he has all the answers. Therefore, we have an interesting conversation, because I do know all the answers! He likes to talk about anything and everything from skydiving to truck driving and from philosophy to money.

"There is money in rental property." I bait the hook.

"I bet there is," says Jeff. "Do people leave anything valuable when they move? Or, do you ever find anything valuable in the houses you buy?"

"You mean like a hidden treasure?" I put the hook in the water.

"Yea like up in an attic or something hid out under

the house. There is no telling what you might find." He bites the hook.

"Are you in a hurry?" I ask.

"Suzie, I don't get in a hurry anymore! I live life one day at a time." He says, with a grin that reminds me of his dad, Marv.

"Would you like to go treasure hunting? Today?"

"Of course!" he exclaims. "Where are we going to find a treasure?" I got him!

In a mysterious way I say, "Let's go see!"

We climb into Jeff's pickup truck. The starter grinds and the motor fires up. "Where to?"

"Let's head towards your mom's house," I say as we back out the drive. "Take County Road 353 and go by the Bolton House." We have been renting out the Bolton House, on and off, for the last three years. I notice there are no cars around.

"Pull into the driveway." He does as I suggest and stops.

The Bolton House looks a little desolate. The yard needs mowing and a mangy black Heinz-57 dog slowly crawls out from under a nearby tree.

I explain, "The house is rented, so I am not legally free to trespass without permission." He looks at me and suspiciously grins. We exit the pickup at the same time.

When we bought the place, it came with a ton of old tools used by Old Man Bolton. After years of pilfering by us and renters, there are still hoes, spades, and some mysterious tools propped up or hanging in the shed and garage.

"Grab that shovel," I order. "Come with me over to the corner of the backyard fence, there might be something buried that we need to find."

Jeff is getting more excited as we climb over the

fence.

"Keep an eye out. I really don't want my tenant to return home, and find us digging in the yard."

"Can we go to jail for this? I don't want to have to call Uncle Mitch!"

"Just dig, right there," I point to the ground, hoping we find something.

On the second scoop of dirt Jeff whispers loudly, "I got something! Looks like a leather strap."

Actually, it was barely under the surface, not buried well at all. Jeff grabs the strap and tugs.

"Whatever is on the other end of this is heavy." More tugging and it does not budge. Jeff digs more and pulls harder. Finally, he falls on his butt as it comes out of the ground and lands between his legs.

"A bowling ball?" It is a dirty bowling ball bag and certainly heavy enough to be a bowling ball! We are both very excited.

"Fill up the hole and let's get out of here," I say. I help cover the area with leaves and stems. We climb back over the fence and make our way to the truck.

"This aint no bowling ball, and if it is, it is the heaviest bowling ball I have ever felt of."

I know what is in the bag and I am elated we found it!

"Let's take it to your house." Jeff lives half a mile past his mother's home.

"What do we have?" Jeff is bursting at the seams. He cannot wait and opens the bag on the tailgate of his truck. "Silver!"

Yes, this is our bag of silver, which Ron dug up after the fire in the high desert of Arizona.

Ron brought this bag to the Bolton House in Texas.

At first, we spent six months at a time in the Texas house. Ron told me where he buried it but, until now, I never saw the exact spot. We seldom talk about the silver. Ron enjoys being secretive about it. I have no idea of the condition of the silver. Since the fire, neither Ron nor I have examined the precious metal. Shortly after he hid it, the Scottsdale lifestyle became our desire. Since we still owned the property, we rented it out and left the buried treasure. This may not sound like a smart thing to do but we did it never-the-less.

Jeff and I empty the contents of the bag onto his asphalt driveway. Sure enough, there is silver, and lots of it! There are melted plastic rolls of silver dollars. Each cylinder contains twenty silver eagles. There are also five one-hundred ounce silver bars! What fun, digging up a buried treasure!

"The plastic is melted to the coins. I have the tools to clean these up," declares Jeff. He returns with the tools and the bathroom scales.

We diligently began to pry away the melted plastic.

"Try not to scratch or damage the coins." Jeff is a stamp collector and knows his way around valuable things. We work several hours cleaning the coins as best we can.

I call Ron, who is in Scottsdale. "Jeff and I have been treasure hunting!"

With Ron on speakerphone, we reveal our project to him. We are laughing and happily telling Ron of our experience. Ron does not appreciate our enthusiasm.

"Why didn't you leave it where it was?" He seems irritated that I took it upon myself to dig up the silver.

"Ron, people are in and out of that house. It was not safe over there. This needs to be in a safety deposit box."

Ron is still not happy, but I don't care. This project

is almost complete.

"Fifty-six pounds!" Jeff looks at the scales and pulls out his calculator. "That's nine-hundred ounces!"

"I just happen to know silver is going for $26.00 an ounce."

A few more taps on the calculator, "Suzie! That's $23,400.00!"

After the cleanup, Jeff helps me carry the treasure to the bank and we put it into a safety deposit box!

So ends the story of THE BURIED TREASURE.

Chapter 31
Another Trip to Texas

"It is going to be a huge thing," I say to Ron as we load the Caravan. "Everything is hush-hush. Everyone is going to Texas for Mother's birthday." She turns eighty-nine February 6, 2008. "Also we need to work on emptying the Bolton House, Glen is giving me the stained glass window he has promised me for years, and I need to pick up my Waterford Crystal vase."

Cleo and Buffy are excited and hopping around. They love to travel and sense that a journey is in the making. They have made the fifteen-hundred mile trip several times. As usual, it starts in the wee hours of the morning. Buffy leaps into the van as soon as the door opens.

"Let's pray," I stop. "When I get back, I forgot my jewelry."

The Accident
Part 7

The Accident has caught up with my life!

To: whom it may concern. A concerned party would be you, if you are reading my story!

To this point, I have been referring to myself as Elizabeth. I'm not sure of the reasoning behind this. At the time I began writing I couldn't bring myself to insert my own name. I had never truly looked back to the life changing events of those days, weeks, or months. Never had I articulated in my mind what took place that February in 2008.

Since writing this story down, getting it out of me, I feel I have finally dealt with the situation that happened. I believe I can now accept the reality of it all. Something therapeutic took place as I wrote. I don't understand the exact reasoning. However, now I believe I can start referring to myself as Suzie.

> I am me,
> Whoever that be!
> Writing my story
> Has set me free!

Chapter 32
Get Thee Behind Me

I will begin writing in the first person! I am Gerry Sue Shamburger Eudy Murphy Cole, (What a name!) Known to most people as Suzie!

After the ride from Hell, things settle down at the Rehab Center in Scottsdale. There is a knock on my door.

"I'm Chris, Twan's friend. We went to church together here in Scottsdale." Chris is sweet and hands me a present, "It's by Joyce Meyer, a Christian author. Her books are full of wisdom and she teaches the Bible."

"Actually, her teachings have been very instrumental in my own Christian growth," I reply.

Soon after Chris leaves, a friend of Connie arrives. If you are a friend of any of my kids, you are a friend of mine. Robin smiles and I remember meeting her. She has a strong Baptist background and her father is a Baptist minister.

"Where is Ron?" Robin immediately asks. "Why isn't he here?"

"Well, he is still sore from the accident and the loss of Cleo has really affected him," I jump to his defense. "He will probably come by later."

Secretly, I am feeling somewhat neglected by Ron. It is not a big crisis. I have learned over the last eighteen years not to expect much from him in the department of mental support. I suppress my disappointment and try not to allow resentment or anger to fester inside. Ron is just Ron! It is not his problem. It is my problem.

During Robin's visit the phone rings and it is

Jerome. I talk about my horrific ride from Midland. Robin picks up the book Chris had brought to me. She reads the cover, thumbs through it and lays it down. She then picks up my *New International Version* Bible. After a comprehensive examination, she closes it and places it back on my bed.

"I have company now. I'll call you back later." I said. "Sorry, it was my son," Robin and I resume our conversation.

"You are a Joyce Myer fan?" she questions. "I see two of her books on your night stand."

"Yes, she has been an inspiration to me for some time."

"Joyce is a television-evangelist," Robin comments.

"She seems to be quite successful in her ministry," I add.

"Her teachings are of the world and not true to the Word of God. As a Christian you must be selective and careful whose teachings you allow in your life." I thought Robin's words were dogmatic and harsh.

"Your Bible", she proceeds to say, "is not the King James version, the one that Christians have always used. These new translations can lead you astray. You shouldn't read them!"

I wish I had said, "Always used? Are you talking about The King James Bible, written in 1611, were there any Christians before 1611?

Have you ever seen an original 1611 King James Bible? I have! It is hard to read much less understand.

I have also seen the Dead Sea Scrolls. God's Word is much older than King James is.

What about the world that does not speak English? Do you have to speak King James English to be a

Christian?

People used King James because it was the only English translation available for many years."

Instead, my heart sinks as I try to comprehend what she is saying. In my delicate condition from the accident, if I were not so feeble minded right now, I could defend my belief in a rational manner.

Preach the Word; be instant in season, out of season; reprove, rebuke, exhort with all longsuffering and doctrine. II Timothy 4:2 (King James Version)

Preach the word: be prepared in season and out of season; correct, rebuke and encourage- with great patience and careful instruction. Second Timothy 4:2 (New International Version)

A Christian Sister has never attacked me.

"I suddenly feel very tired. You can leave." This leaves me confused.

Doubt: I lie there and began to question my belief system. Have I been drawing from sources other than that of God? Was I studying the wrong translation of the Bible? How can this be?

I thought I was strong in the faith. I thought my relationship with God was special, that it was true and built on a solid foundation. What am I thinking? How did I let this happen? My mind is in absolute torment.

Doubt: He who doubts is like a wave on the sea, blown and tossed by the wind. That man should not think he will receive anything from the Lord; he is a double-minded man, unstable in all he does. James 1:6-8 (NIV)

Doubt: Does she know something about Ron that I do not? He used to have a gambling problem.

Single Vision is a theory in which we see God in all things. Where is my Single Vision?

"Ha, ha, ha," I hear a faint laugh and look up to the corner of my room.

"Who are you?" as unbelievable as it sounds, I see a demon.

"Ha, ha, ha," is all he or it will say. It looks like the devils portrayed in painting and writings. Only this demon is small. In the upper corner of my room, it is wiggling and sneering at me. He looks like he is ready to attack.

I realize what is happening and panic! I am under attack by the forces of evil! I know what to do. This requires prayer and lots of it. The demon must be rebuked! I fumble with the phone, and call Saint Lolo.

"Mother, you've got to pray for me," I exclaim as soon as she answers the phone. There is no time for greetings or idle chitchat.

"Of course I'll pray, I always pray for you, you've come so far . . ."

I interrupt her, "No Mother, you've got to pray hard and pray now! I'm under attack and it is bad!"

Mother promptly begins to pray, "Lord Jesus, cover Suzie with your protection. I rebuke thee Satan and your demons. In the name of Jesus I command thee to be gone."

I hear those words as the phone drops and I drift off into a deep sleep.

I awake lying on a gurney in the emergency room at Scottsdale Memorial Hospital! Ron is standing beside the bed and nurses are busily working over me.

"Let's get two IVs started and two units of blood." I hear someone in the distance saying. I have no idea what is happening.

Chapter 33
The Setback

"You've had a setback," Ron reveals. "Here is the surgeon, Dr. Ferrari, he will explain."

"The surgery in Texas was a success. Dr. Sawyer actually saved your life, but the small intestines did not heal properly. They have now perforated. More surgery must be performed immediately."

As I lay there waiting, the pain is worse than before. Little did I know this new ailment would be far more traumatic than the past three weeks.

"The problem is we do not know how much of the small bowel needs to be removed," Dr. Ferrari tells Ron. "I have studied and I know what needs to be done. The technique is used in wartime battle injuries. We will induce a coma so she will be resting throughout the procedure. We will have to leave her open and visually inspect the bowel to remove any necrotic or dead tissue. When we see the bowel working completely, we will close her back up. She will be the first woman in the United States to be given this particular surgical procedure."

"Is she going to be alright?" ask Ron.

"Unfortunately, this is a slow process and may take days or a week to make sure everything is working. We do not want to wake her up until all is functioning."

"Is she going to be alright?" questions Ron again.

"There is a high risk. It all depends on how much we have to remove and if there is an abdominal infection."

For a long 32 days, I am in a medically induced coma. I lay on my back with my abdomen cut and extended open. Every couple of days, they take me back to the operating room and the surgery team examines my intestines. When there is evidence that another inch or foot of intestine is no good; they cut off the bad gut and repack me with sterile sponges. With my abdomen left open, I return to the intensive care unit. Day after a day we go through the same dance again.

I have vague recollections of those 32 days: Dreams and hallucinations, stuck in a wheelchair, trying to get somewhere; someone helping me, talking to me. When I realize it is a real voice, I cannot talk back. I am frustrated. I cannot express myself.

One other memory is hearing my cousin, Lane, speaking to me as she rubs my arm soothingly saying, "Breathe in….Breathe out……Breathe in…..Breathe out."

"We have done all we can," says Dr. Ferrari. "We have extracted as much of the intestine as possible. We have closed her up. The rest is up to God."

I started out with about twenty feet of small bowel. Now I have eighteen . . . INCHES. My life depends on the nutrients injected into my veins.

"Here is your supper," the nurse pronounces as she hangs the Total Parenteral Nutrition (TPN) on the IV pole. It is a plastic bag full of vitamins, minerals and whatever I need to stay alive. "You may as well get used to it. Honey, you will be getting this supper for the rest of your life."

The function of the small intestines is to absorb nutrients, minerals, and necessary vitamins. The intestines have little feelers in them. Each little feeler performs its individual function; each feeler pulls in their particular nutrient. Since most of my feelers are gone, it will be very hard for my body to absorb what I need to live.

"Maybe you should call in the family," says Dr. Ferrari.

Chapter 34
Wakeup Little Suzie

"Ryan! You were in Dallas for your back surgery and now you look great!" I wake up to see Ryan and Sally standing by my bedside.

"You were not supposed to walk for several months!" He is smiling and standing upright, straighter than he ever stood before. I am mystified.

"It has been three months," Sally says. "You both went into the hospital at the same time, three months ago."

Still in constant pain, I am moved to Scottsdale South Hospital and put on a floor for recovering patients. The diarrhea continues and I depend on caregivers to keep me in fresh diapers. Every time they get around to cleaning me, immediately, I poop again!

"Now I know why babies cry with dirty diapers," I tell the nurse's aide. "Minutes seem like hours." This process continues for weeks. My rear is raw and feels like it is on fire all the time.

"It is a continuous, excruciation pain," I tell Mitch. He and Mother flew in earlier in the week.

My children come on weekends. By this time, everyone, including me, is worn out! It has been two months since the accident. This was however, my first real awareness of what had happened since arriving back into Arizona.

Mother and Mitch return to Texas and give their report of my condition.

Sister to the Rescue

Perry arrives with determination. I, on the other hand, am not so determined. My attitude is not good. I hurt. I do not have the personal drive to get well, nor am I willing to commit to trying.

"I wish I had a sister like yours," one nurse says. "She keeps us on our toes and knows what we are supposed to do." They are amazed that she was willing to be such a strong support system for me.

On the other hand, Ron comes by for a few minutes each day, not to see how I am doing, but to fill me in on information about the world outside.

My world did not go far outside my room. They install an intravenous port just above my right breast, to do the TPN feedings. The port is fragile and the insert has to be changed weekly. This process requires a very sterile environment.

On the third week, I realize a new the team is doing the procedure. They do not seem to know what they are doing. I am still weak and although I know they are not doing it correctly, I say not a word! They take over an hour to do what usually takes fifteen minutes. By the end of the week, my blood is infected.

"There is poison in your blood," the doctor tells me.

A new batch of doctors starts to work on my new batch of problems. Infection, nutrition, infusion, and confusion seem to sum up my life for the next year.

Perry and I move from one rehab facility to another. Wherever I go there is another faithful follower! Marion (Mimi) Miller, my adopted sister-in-law, consistently appears in my room at six in the evening. Mimi fights the traffic all the way across town to visit and pray with me every day! She takes home pajamas or anything that needs to be cleaned. Her daily prayers are beautiful.

"Therefore confess your sins to each other and pray for each other so that you may be healed. The prayer of a righteous person is powerful and effective." James 5:15 (NIV) I could never thank Mimi enough for her dedication to my case.

"You have to walk by yourself before you can leave the hospital," Perry insists. "It's been four long months and I'm ready to go home."

"I can't. Lying in bed with limited nutrition for so long has made my muscles contract and dry up. My feet are even misshaped. I depend on a walker. I slowly creep a few steps and then I fight to sit or go back to bed."

"We have had enough of this pity party," continues Perry. "We are going outside." The physical therapist and my sister, Perry, take me for a trip completely around the hospital. I whine, even cry, as they force me to walk. There is a belt around my waist and they hold it from behind. All the way around that huge building we go. As we come around to the final stretch, we stop.

"Suzie, it is decision time," my therapist knelt beside me. "You have a choice. You can give up and waste away in a hospital bed. Or, you can be the answer to many prayers and get well."

"I want to get well!"

"Then walk!" She and Perry step back and leave me standing alone. I take one-step and then another.

"I am going to be well again!" My tears of pain and despair turn to tears of joy with these first few steps.

"You are ready for home health," says the doctor a week later. Reluctantly, I take the challenge and go to our home in Scottsdale and Perry finally returns to Texas.

My care is a continuous drain and very time consuming. Ron is nervous and acts as though taking care of me is beneath him. Nurses come to hook up the TPN every evening. The physical therapist comes in three times a week.

"Mom, we've decided you are regressing! You are not able to take care of yourself and Ron surely isn't helping matters." Twan made the phone call.

"I know. Ron stormed out of the house this morning angry, saying he wasn't going to spend the rest of his life playing nurse to me," I confirm her worries.

"David is in Scottsdale and will be flying back to California on Friday. He can help you make the trip. Connie says you can live with her and Brad. You'll have your own room." Twan tells me. "I live only a few blocks away and will help with the load. If you are ever going to get well, you can't stay there!"

"Are you sure? I hate to impose on y'all, but I can't go on like this much longer."

"We've got it all planned out!" This is a welcome phone call for me.

By Friday, Twan and Connie have contacted doctors and made appointments for me. My home health care coordinates with California so there is no interruption with any of my health care.

"Yes Mother," I call Lolo to tell her of the change. "It is amazing. Connie and Twan have it all under control! My TPN was waiting for me at Connie's when I got here. Home Health Care came in and taught her how to hook me up. Twan has my doctor appointments all lined up and will take me to them. I feel so much better about my recovery now."

This new phase of recovery consist of my living with Connie and Brad again. I remembered my illness of 2003. This time is just as challenging. Their household normalcy is on hold as the Lober family dedicates their time to my getting well!

My body and mind are beginning to heal. I realize a great deal of time has passed.

"It has been six months since I've dealt with the household books. Knowing Ron, I doubt that he has stepped up to the plate." I tell Connie as I log into our online banking. "Where is the money?"

It is evident that our banking accounts were drained during my illness. Not only is the savings account almost gone, but also there is a new sixteen thousand dollars credit card debt!

"The insurance took care of the medical bills! Where did the rest of the money go?" I questioned the computer screen. "I see Ron made the association payments and paid the utilities, and he paid for a big screen television! Where are the rent money deposits?"

Connie sits down with a long expression on her face as she begins. "Mom, Ron was gambling while you were in the hospital. We suspected this was happening. I hacked into your bank accounts and we saw that he was draining everything. Brad confronted Ron and that was all we could do."

After eating those sour grapes, I discover that Ron gave one of our credit cards to someone we both trusted. I got a credit card statement saying we owe sixteen thousand dollars!

With this news, I felt sick, even violated. This all transpired while I was fighting for my life.

The credit card company assures me that I am liable for the debt. They ask me to prosecute, but I do not feel it is the right thing to do.

"I promise to pay it back in full," the trusted one said.

NOTE (The trusted one did make a few payments. I am the only person who believes that one day he will come to me and pay his bill. Only time will tell.)

Chapter 35
Slow Road to Recovery

I am supposed to be getting better as my hair falls out, I develop shingles, and I end up in the emergency room several times.

"Cedar Sinai Hospital and UCLA in Los Angeles," my doctors recommend. Both are inconvenient and for naught. They did not want to deal with my problem nor me.

Meanwhile, I continue to receive TPN each night. Nurses come several times a week for blood test and therapy. Once per week, the port in my chest has to be cleaned and the insert changed by a nurse.

Christmas 2008, I make the big announcement. "This has been a great Christmas and I believe this California group is about burned out! I think I am well enough to go to East Texas and spend a couple of months with Perry. She is a perfect caregiver."

With nursing arrangements made, I am back in Winona. Perry exceeds her sisterly duties and again, is my health care person and cheerleader.

"I want to have a get-together! I would like a special time to speak to all my East Texas friends and loved ones who have been praying for me. I want to thank them personally and praise God!"

"We can meet in the back room of the Back Porch,"

says Perry. Her daughter, Marlee owns and operates the restaurant.

Perry and Marlee get it together! On a Sunday afternoon, over twenty people are praising God for the miracle of prayer and the miracle of my life. I Praise God that I am here to celebrate!

Today February 15, 2009, is exactly one year since the accident. I am not completely well, but prayers are still being spoken and I am improving every day. As Perry Jo said back there in Midland, "Don't pray that she will just live, pray that she will completely recover!"

As my itching shingles subsided my itching to travel returned. "I can't stay here forever and I'm getting anxious to get back to normal living. I miss Scottsdale and I want to go back," I declare to Perry. "I've learned how to do the nightly TPN by myself and I think I'm strong enough to take Ron on."

An air flight from Tyler to Dallas, to Phoenix and I am home! Ron picks me up at the airport and we begin life together again. It has been over a year since the accident and we have spent very little time together.

Ron has grown accustomed to single living and he likes it.

"Where is the hall tree?" My cross wall, it has been completely rearranged to a different wall. This just does not seem like my house at all. Even my clothes, which were in the master bedroom, have been moved into the guest bedroom.

Ron replaced Cleo with another dog, Boudreau, a Papillion. He is very devoted to both dogs and allows them to rule the household.

I go into the kitchen, "Where are the glasses?" I question after opening several cabinets. Ron jumps ahead of me and acts offended as I look for things where they have always been. "Nothing is in its old place."

"I didn't know if you were ever coming back," explains Ron.

I go to the den and start to sit down and Boudreau is lying in my chair.

"Get up," I say in my dog commanding voice. Boudreau and Ron give me a look that does not sit right with me. "Do you wish I hadn't survived the accident? You would have our home all to yourself. Have I been replaced by a dog?"

Grandson Bash graduated high school in May. Brad gave him a wonderful present. Brad took Bash, his best friend, my granddaughter Dalys, Connie, Leola, Ben and me on a trip to Maui, Hawaii. We all enjoyed a full week living the tropical good life. I was still on TPN and this had to be sent in a special temperature controlled atmosphere. We were at the hotel less than an hour when Leola fell off playground equipment and broke her arm. Other than those two complications, the trip was fabulous. I smiled as I remembered reading Brads promise of the trip.

California Here We Come

After three months of trying to resume life in Scottsdale; Twan, Connie and Jerome are fearful that Ron is not helping me enough. "Why don't you two move to California so we can help?"

I am pleased with that suggestion so they assist us in

finding an affordable place in Oxnard, California. We make the move. I remain on TPN and continue having home health care on a weekly basis.

Perry's daughter, Morgan, moves into the co-op in Arizona. "This is for one year," is our agreement.

California is so inviting. I love entertaining a lot of company. There is so much to see and do. Mother spends over a month with us. Ron seems perturbed, yet I do not allow it to deter my zeal for life.

The weather in Oxnard averages a perfect 66 degrees all year long. The beautiful Pacific beaches are less than three miles away. My kids and grand ones live only thirty minutes away. Life in California should be wonderful. However, that is not the case concerning the life of Ron and Suzie! Our household is full of tension.

A team of doctors decide that my intestines and the scars are healed enough to have Abdomen Reconstruction Surgery.

The surgery goes well. In six weeks, I have fully recovered, as far as the doctors are concerned. I am still on intravenous TPN. TPN forever! I start to do some traveling, although the TPN must be ordered ahead and waiting at my destination. It is the same process wherever I go, which is a lot of trouble.

While I am visiting Perry, I make an unscheduled visit to the doctor. He shows an interest about the TPN port on my chest.

"I will be on the TPN the rest of my life," I explain to him.

"You should try eating," the doctor casually said. "It may run straight through you, but at least you will get the enjoyment of tasting food!"

"The doctors told me I will never be able to eat or digest food." I argue.

"Why not? Everything seems to work," the doctor responds.

Perry and I give each other a startled look. "Why not?" I already have continual diarrhea even though I eat nothing. I have not considered eating to see what happens.

That moment is the start of a miracle, which eventually gets me off TPN! My body starts to absorb the nutrients it needs, I need! Two years after the accident, I am no longer dependent on an IV for my supper. Again, the doctors are amazed.

More Troubled Waters

Ron is dissatisfied with California and me! He is gambling more and more. He stays in Las Vegas for days at a time, or he drives sixty-five miles north to a Native American reservation and the Chumash Casino. California has casinos too!

I am waiting for Ron when he enters the door. "You've been gone all week-end! Online banking says you've drained our savings again! How does it feel to come home with not only empty pockets, but an empty bank account as well?"

In twenty-two years of marriage, Ron has only apologized to me one time. He begins what looks like an apology! "Yes, I know I've messed up. I was just one pull away from a royal flush. I know that machine was about to hit. But, I ran out of money. Damn it, I know if I had just a little more to feed the machine, I could have been a winner!" Ron is convinced he could have won and he blames me for not having enough money to make him a winner.

"Looks like we both lost. I have had enough and we are broke! You need to admit your gambling problem and try to get yourself fixed." I am thoroughly disgusted at this point.

For the second time in our marriage, Ron did ask for forgiveness.

"I'm sorry. I know I need help. I have been through this before." We locate gamblers anonyms.

"I don't need help," Ron returns from his first meeting very irritated. "Those people in that meeting are busy bodies. One of them said I reminded him of his alcoholic father. Now what right did he have to be discussing that?" Ron never returns to a meeting and he gambles every time he gets any money.

I resume the business of renting houses, which demands a lot of attention. I am still mentally exhausted from the wreck and can use some help. Ron makes life unbearable when it comes to business.

Turmoil dominates our lives. We have lived together in California for almost a year. Ron insists on moving Morgan out of the Arizona co-op.

"But she has two months left on our agreement," I argue.

"I'm moving back to Arizona," says Ron. "Get Morgan out of there." We give Morgan two weeks to move. With a rented pickup, we move all of Ron's belongings back to Arizona.

Leaving Arizona without Ron is traumatic for me. Driving away from our co-op, I began to weep. I do not cry often but the floodgates open and sob uncontrollably.

Unable to concentrate on my driving, I have to pull over to the side of the road for fifteen minutes or so. Never, in my entire life, do I remember ever crying that hard.

We did not plan to divorce. The intention was that I would continue to pay the bills and send him an allowance to live on.

"How can I trust you?" he asks.

"Trust me?" That makes me so mad I insist we get a divorce.

The property is not divided equally. I agree to Ron getting all of his retirement and social security. I had three rental houses before I met him so I insist on having three when the divorce is final. We agree that we will each keep the place where we live and that whoever lives the longest will get the other piece of property. Ron gave out the credit card, but I assume the sixteen thousand dollar debt.

Chapter 36
Roy Dies

One of the good, or bad, things about cell phones is that you can receive a call anytime and anywhere. The phone rings just after I sit down for a manicure. My manicurist, Mia, has removed the old polish and graciously waits for me to answer this call. I see Nancy, Roy's sister, on the caller ID. It has been over six months since we have spoken. We call only on special occasions.

"Hello."

"Suzie, Nancy here. I am calling to let you know that Roy had a massive stroke last night and he is in intensive care at Medical Center Hospital in Tyler. I don't think he is going to live long. I just thought you needed to know." She tells me Roy was having health problems over the past few months. From our Christmas conversation, I knew Roy weighed over 300 pounds and looked like Santa Claus with a long, bushy flowing beard. Nancy closed with, "I don't really know much more than that but I will keep you updated."

After my nails were done, I returned home to begin the phone calls.

"Connie, your Aunt Nancy called and told me that Roy had a stroke. He is in intensive care and not expected to live much longer." Connie was three when he left us and I doubt this will bother her too much. She has only seen him once since he left thirty-seven years ago.

"Twan, Aunt Nancy called and said Roy had a stroke and is in intensive care. He's not expected to survive." I feel this may upset Twan. She was close to Roy during the first five years of her life. She is the only one of the children who sought him out over the years. When Dalys, her first child, was several months old, Twan found Roy and took Dalys for a visit. It was not what she expected.

"Mom, come get me. Georgia is crazy. She is making potions and expects me to give them to Dalys. She is a gypsy, she speaks gypsy and she tries to make me speak gypsy. It's crazy here! Come get me now!"

In Twan's mind, she wanted to spend a week with her "DAD" and he would see and love his new blood granddaughter. All of the years of heartache would disappear. After that visit, Twan very seldom mentions Roy.

"Jerome, Nancy Eudy called and said Roy has suffered a stroke and isn't expected to live." Jerome was one day old when Roy made that infamous stroll into the "Green Frog" and met Georgia. I do not expect a lot of reaction from him.

"Mom, this news has me feeling very mixed up!" Connie calls early this morning and she is emotional. "I don't know what to do. I feel like I want to go and be by his side. Though I don't even know Roy, I am really sad. I want him to know that I care about him. Would it be stupid for me to fly all the way from California to Texas to see the man who deserted us? He is my biological father you know." This reaction surprises me.

Twan calls with a cold and callous attitude, "I've reached out to Roy several times during my adult life and he has never really given me the time of day. I don't care if he does die. It won't bother me one bit." This reaction is totally opposite of what I expect from Twan.

There is no response from Jerome, just as I anticipated.

I have a full schedule today, which includes a Ladies Bible Study with a big luncheon.

"Suzie, Roy died early this morning. No arrangements have been made but I'll let you know later," says Nancy.

During the Bible Study, Twan calls and asks a question which I quickly answer and we hung up.

Late in the afternoon and after the whirlwind of activities, I notify the kids with news of Roy's death.

"Twan, I forgot to tell you when you called today, Roy died early this morning." There is silence. I fumble around with a few more words and we say good-bye.

"Connie, there won't be time for you to go to Roy. He died early this morning. I'm sorry that you're upset about this and I wish I could take away your sadness. But this is a sad situation you'll have to deal with."

"Jerome, Roy died. I doubt that you'll get that big inheritance you always jokingly say Roy owes you kids!" Jerome never has much to say on the topic of Roy.

Later in the evening I call Connie back wondering how we should express our condolences. I am pleasantly surprised. Connie has already contacted her cousins in Texas. Roy was their uncle and she decided to reach out to them. Connie is writing Roy a letter. Cousin Gwen has told her she will read it to Roy. Connie sits down at the computer.

Dear Roy …

Love That Social Media

Meanwhile Twan is brewing up a stink! Social Media has a way of spreading news and thoughts FAST.

Twan dearest goes to Facebook and makes a post.

"My Dad died today and Mom let me know
by saying, "Oh, I forgot to tell you, your dad
died today."

The sympathetic comments pour in. Instantly I became the evil heartless mother. People who did not know me blasted me and consoled Twan. Others, who I thought knew me, added fuel to the fire.

Eventually Connie comments on Twan's post:
"Roy Eudy was our birth father, he
abandoned us and we were raised by a very
nice man who adopted us. Our last name is
Murphy"

I doubt that the first thirty-two commentators ever saw Connie's fact.

Jerome remains visibly unmoved by this episode.

As for me, Roy's death makes me very sad. I praise God for eleven wonderful years of marriage. If things had gone differently, we would have ended up a happy little redneck family living on a farm in East Texas. Roy was my first love and truthfully the love of my life. Because of him, I have three beautiful children. I see a sparkle of Roy in each one. Who could ask for anything more?

At the graveside service, Cousins Gwen and Lisa along with Aunt Nancy stood at the foot of the coffin. Gwen read Connie's letter aloud and then placed it beside Roy. Tears were shed for a life that was.

Dear Roy,
I am typing this letter to tell you a few

things about me and what I wonder about you.

I am a mother of three, one son who is in the Air Force and two young ones that will be returning to school next week.

I wish I had known you. I wish I knew your mannerisms and your sense of humor. I do not know why you made the choices you did. It is not for me to understand.

I wish for you, that your life was rich and you had someone to love and made you smile. It is sad that I could not love you and make you laugh, because I'm pretty funny, and so are Twan and Jerome! We, your children, love each other very much and all three of us are very close. We talk, text and visit all the time.

Twan was the most hurt by your leaving. I think it is because she knew you the longest. She still, to this day has not figured out how to love men. It is very hard for her.

FYI, I had a wonderful father (Paul Murphy) who loves me and has raised me. He's a nice guy and has never turned his back on us. Don't get me wrong, he can drive us crazy at times, but we really love that man.

It is sad, because we had enough love for you as well. I realize now that you are gone and with God, that my chance to get to know you is over, to look at you, look into your eyes, to talk to you and hear your voice.

I want to know how you sounded, how you handled pain, anger, and happiness. I know I am a piece of you, and nothing can change that.

All this time I felt like I was waiting for you. I could have taken that step. I could have reached out to you. I guess I felt like a child, always feeling like the child. With the feeling, you cannot reach out unless the parent reaches for you. Maybe children, maybe I, was afraid of another rejection from that parent.

I wish I could have seen you age - and you could have seen me and my kids grow up. Life passes so quickly. We all live in the moment and don't pay attention to what we are doing to others, and even to ourselves.

The only memory I have of you is at Papaw's funeral, I did not know who you were. As Mom and I were leaving, you came and asked who I was, and you hugged me. You held me so long and so tight, I couldn't breathe. All I could think was, "Who is this man and why is he hugging me so hard and long?" As we drove off Mom looked at me and said, "That man was your father." I was sad, because I would have hugged you back, just as long and hard as you had held me.

Why do people do what they do? Why would you not reach for us? Why would we not reach for you? These things I do not understand. And here I sit, wondering who you were - and why I never got a piece of you.

Roy, my father, I send loving thoughts to you and your family. I pray one day I can hug you back and see your smile. I hope you can look down from Heaven, see your children and know us the way we all wish you had, all our lives.

I do not think you were a bad man. I do not know you enough to decide such a thing. I do know, as a father, you were not so great. That is mean, but it is true.

I wanted to come be with you in your final days, but I didn't know if that was where I should be. I send you my love - as it was always there. I send kind and sweet thoughts - as I always did. Go be with God and rest. I'm sorry we never knew one another. I do thank you for giving me a sister and brother whom I love and cherish every day.

I'm sorry I didn't reach for you. I'm sorry you didn't reach for me.

Forever your daughter,
Connie

Chapter 37
Reality of Divorce!

"This is God's opportunity!" I tell my cousins, June and Sara. We are having lunch at a The Tea Room in Tyler. "My social security is less than $500.00 a month and the money from rent houses is not dependable. Sometimes the expenses outweigh the profits! It will be interesting to see how God pulls this one off." They agree and give concerned smiles.

"Gerry Sue, I see here you've been married THREE times," says the social security agent, his eyebrows raised.

"Yes, I know, is there something wrong with that?" It is May 2011 and my divorce will soon be final.

"No, but you were married to each one of your husbands over ten years, that is very unusual. Good news, though. You can draw from any one of the three. Let's see, who has the largest benefit for you. I also see that your first husband died last month."

"Yes, I am aware of that."

"Good news again, Gerry Sue! You can draw benefits from Mr. Eudy's social security. His survivor benefits are considerably higher. I'll go back and see how much I can get for you."

In a few minutes, the gentleman returns with a smile on his face. He writes a figure down on a piece of paper. "Here, this is the new amount which will be automatically deposited into your account the month after your divorce is final."

"Thank you," I look at the figure and tell the gentleman again, "Thank you."

When I get into my car, I take another look at the number written on the piece of paper. I cannot believe my eyes! Not in my wildest dreams did I think God, through the US government, would take care of me in this way. This is amazing! The figure is over four times the amount I was previously getting. "Ye- ha!"

Single again! Three marriages behind me, 65 years old and free, free once more! There are several ways to look at this. Either I am a three time looser, or I am three times better off. I have lived a good life, with little strife. The last year has been stressful. Therefore, I conclude that right now I am good-to-go, free again to enjoy this, the final chapter of my life.

I live an active lifestyle consisting of travel and church activities. I spend much time in East Texas visiting family and realize how fortunate I am to have a living mother in her nineties. I share much of my time with my children and grand ones.

I realize God is blessing me daily! Yes, I have been and continue to be truly blessed!

"Without faith it is impossible to please God, because anyone who comes to him must believe that he exists and that he rewards those who earnestly seek him." Hebrews 11:6 (NIV)

Chapter 38
Ron's Final Days

Monday, December 16, 2013 is an early rise and I rush to the Ventura County courthouse to meet my daughter. Twan is pleading her case before the judge requesting child support for her daughter, Alyssa. Twan has been divorced for over three years and Alyssa will be eighteen in eight months. Twan feels her Ex should bear at least a little responsibility for their teen daughter.

The court hearing is short and Twan does not have to go back to work.

"How about a little mother-daughter time?" We plan for lunch and do the things girls like to do. Going to the AT&T store is our second stop. As we are getting out of the car, my phone rings.

"Suzie, I'm calling to tell you some bad news. Ron has cancer in his liver, kidneys and bloodstream. It is in the last stages and he's in hospice." I put the phone on speaker so Twan could help me adsorb the shocking news. Candy Wise, our neighbor in Scottsdale, continued the report. "Ron has been confirmed to have inoperable cancer. He was diagnosed with it in late November and now he has very little time!" Candy proceeded to say,

"Is there anything we can do?" I ask.

"Ron asked me to not tell you, or anyone else, until he is dead and I have his ashes."

The last time I saw or talked to Ron was about six months ago. We have remained cordial although he complains that I got more in the divorce than I should have.

His feelings are unfounded and false. The property was divided in his favor. With his obsession for gambling, Ron did not managed his money well at all. While I, on the other hand, was my usual, obsessive frugal self. I have managed fine while he was struggling financially.

Actually, I complain just the opposite.

Since our divorce in 2010, Ron has never attempted to contact me. I check in with him, filling him in on the latest activities of grand kids and members of the family. Little seven-year-old Leola went to spend a few hours with him. Although Ron is not "blood kin", everyone on my side of the family considers Ron a family member. Twenty-two years in our clan pretty well makes you permanently grafted. I try to stay in contact with his children, since I am their step-mom. I am not one who can turn love on or off, like a water faucet.

Twan and I cut our excursion short. I realize I have an obligation. It is only a week until Christmas and I do not know how much longer Ron will live. I need to notify his children. My mind goes into overdrive.

I inform Ron's children of their dad's health. Cindy and Greg, along with Ron's first wife, Donna, plan to fly to Arizona to visit him. The next week they fly into Phoenix and spend a day visiting Ron at the hospice facility.

"The report is a good one," says Greg. I was holding my breath. I knew Ron's attitude might assault us all. With his narcissist personality, nobody can live up to his expectations.

"He was fully coherent when we visited with him. Dad was pleased to see everyone. We talked and it offered closure for everyone involved." Greg explained. "Even Alan (Donna's present husband) went along on the whirlwind trip to Arizona and back in a day!"

A California Christmas came and went. It was nice to be around my kids. For some reason Christmas seemed different. It lacked the reverence it should have had.

Candy keeps me informed of Ron's condition. I do not know where I stand with him now that he is sick. He has legally turned all of his affairs over to Candy, with the request of not telling anyone until she has his ashes. I think he might not want to see me.

I cannot imagine Ron dying alone. His daughter predicted years ago, "You will die all alone and a very lonely man." It is as though he willed himself to make that prediction come true! I cannot let it happen.

"Do you mind if I come down?" I ask Ron doubting his approval.

"Of course," he answers, acting as though we never had a problem. He has acted this way every time I have seen him since divorce. On the other hand, he lets everyone else know how very bitter he is.

On New Year's Eve, 2014, I make the long drive to Glendale, Arizona.

I drive directly to Living Waters Care Home. They greet and lead me to Ron's room. Ron is lying there, peacefully asleep. In November his saliva glands stopped working so he can neither eat nor swallow food. Ron looks like bones covered with skin. He is very weak.

I bend over him and say in my loud stern voice, "Wake up Ron, you can't sleep all day!"

"Wow, you nurses are getting prettier!" He shakes his head nodding back and forth blinking his eyes.

"Ron, it's me Suzie, I'm not a nurse."

"I thought you were coming tomorrow. I am so glad to see you. It is good to see anyone I know." He continues to talk and the conversation drifts to Candy Wise. "She has been wonderful, handling my finances and doing the things I can't."

"What about the dogs?" I ask.

"That is the best thing of all, she adopted Buffy and Boudreaux! She loves them so much. Would you believe she has house trained them?" (Ron could not accomplish this task during the entire five years of Boudreaux's life.)

"I'll be back," I have to tell Ron several times before I can break loose and go to Clare's house. That is where I stay when I am in town.

New Year's Day, Clare and I go to spend time with Ron. We talk, joke and laugh a lot.

"Today you are another Great Grandpa!"

Chris, Greg's son, had a baby boy. His name is Keaton Cole. Look!" I show him the small photo on my Smartphone. Ron smiles a wide grin.

"We need to go," Clare or I would say.
"Please stay a little longer," Ron insists, almost begging.

Thursday, I bring an enlarged picture of his new great grandson and put it on the bedside table.

"Suzie," he reaches toward me. His mouth is dry and his words are a bit muffled, but his voice strong. I can tell he is serious.

Again, "Suzie, I've had a lot of time to think. I realize the very best and most important event in my life was meeting you. You led me to God. Had it not been for you I would be in a mess. I would not have turned to God."

Of course, this makes me smile with relief. It answers the big question that lays heavy on my heart. I silently praise the Lord for Ron's confession to me. He is earnest and sincere about his renewed faith, even until his last coherent words. He had professed Christ for years, but he did not experience the joy or the benefits of the Christian living, until now!

Friday and Saturday, Ron's health continues to decline.

"A good name is better than good ointment, and the day of one's death is better than the day of one's birth." My brother Mitch has written several books. His latest, *Music (For the Not So Rich and*

Famous) & Funerals, has a chapter that refers to Ecclesiastes 7:1 and the Wisdom of Solomon. Mitch goes on to quote verses, which express the good side of death. We as Christians should be familiar with these scriptures and, if we really believe them, rejoice with those who are dying. My family has always had this attitude about death and yet it seems to be a strange one to many, even among Christians.

"Read that chapter again," Ron asked me over and over.

Once, while reading, I notice his eyes are closed. I pause, "Are you even listening?"

With his eyes still closed, Ron replies, "Yes." He is listening and trying to absorb it. Ron is actually excited about his soon-to-be death!

"I am ready to go. Why is God taking so long?"

We discuss Bible truths about Heaven and he would relax.

As I walk into the room Sunday morning, he almost shouts in a jovial yet stern voice, "The next time you talk to God, tell him to hurry up!"

"Hurry up for what?" I question.

"You know what I want. I'm ready to go to Heaven!"

We laugh and I tell him, "You have to get worse before you can get better." We pray together.

We enjoy conversations. His usual negativity, bitterness and anger ceases and he seems to finally enjoy life! He is not looking back; rather he becomes obsessed with his future in

Heaven!

He is completely bedridden. He is very talkative. Toward the end of the day, he begins to switch subjects in the middle of a sentence, making it hard to follow his conversation. As I leave tonight, I can tell Ron is beginning to "check out."

"Ron is in his last stage of life," the hospice nurse informs me the following day. *I had no idea what a long, grueling process this last stage would be.*

I text Ron's two children, and tell them of their fathers condition.

I feel the need to remain with him and Living Waters suggest I sleep in the extra bed in Ron's room. Sleeping in my tight jeans is not very comfortable. Whenever I doze off Ron wakes me with loud moans.

"I couldn't do it!" he calmly confesses after a time of quietness.

"Couldn't do what?" I asked.

"Kill myself. I could not take my own life. The Bible says I wouldn't go to Heaven. Doesn't it?"

"Well," I begin, "I don't actually think it says that. Jesus paid for our sins on the cross. It is rejecting Jesus that sends one to hell. I've also come to believe we need to trust in, rely on, and give our lives to Christ daily in order to live the fulfilled life of a victorious Christian".

Ron adds, "I do know that Saul killed himself. Still, I just could not do it. I've always thought I would be able to take my life whenever I wanted to."

With that, we both agree and we are glad he had not followed through with his lifelong plan.

I pick Greg up at the bus station around noon on Tuesday. He visits his dad for a while and I make a fast trip to Clare's house to clean up and get my PJ's.

On Wednesday, Greg and I spend the day at Ron's side. Ron is not coherent, but when we hold his hand, talk loud to him or kiss him on the forehead, he responds favorably. We reminisce about Ron and our experiences. There is no denying; Ron has not spent his life, "winning friends and influencing people!" Those who know him well will agree.

"It is time to start the morphine," the caregiver tells Greg and me. "Once this process begins, his time will be short."

"If he has to go, let's do it as quick and as painless as possible," Greg and I agree. I spend the night, but not in jeans. I wear my pajamas this time. We both have a very peaceful night's sleep.

"It is time again," says the nurse. The hourly shot of morphine is administered. They gradually increase the dosage until they reached the maximum they can give. Greg and I remain in his room thinking Ron will go soon. It is a long day. Nighttime finds Ron still lingering.

"He looks like death warmed over," I mumble to myself. The night seems endless. The peacefulness ends.

"Ohhhh Ohhhhh!" He screams loud dreadful screeches every fifteen to twenty minutes. The sounds express excruciating pain and torment. I hold his hand and rub his bony arm, which settles him temporarily.

Neither he nor I had considered there would be such suffering before he actually died. Until Wednesday, Ron had experienced very little pain. I asked him regularly and he would pat his chest and abdomen (where the pain patches were) saying through muffled words, "Not at all! I feel fine."

January 10, that is today! This little escapade is getting to be a bit longer than I had anticipated! It's Friday afternoon, Greg has come and we are in Ron's room simply being here. That is our job for now. We agree, when Ron starts jerking, moaning or changing his demeanor, we rub his arms, say kind words, or just do anything to emphasize that he is not alone.

"He can go at any time," says the nurse. "It might be tonight, tomorrow or whenever. There is no way of knowing for sure. There is no set pattern which must be followed."

So what happened to that prediction made by nurses and caregivers, about his time being short? Is this considered short? Here it is three days later and Ron is still fading away, oh so slowly!

That's just like God! Keeping us on our toes and depending on Him to let us know when the time is right. Science has not figured it out! Only God knows. He has known since Ron's birth exactly how and when he would leave his earthly mortal body and slip into immortality, wearing his robe of righteousness forevermore! (PTL)

Connie and Twan are on their way from California.

My family back in Texas, California family, Candy, Carolyn, Clare and numerous others continue to keep in touch. Their prayers and concern are appreciated.

"His breathing has changed," whispers Greg.

We get closer and look intently at Ron. We realize he is breathing his last breaths! What a surreal moment. We both gasp as tears fill our eyes. We just look at one another and then back to Ron. He is dying! His chest stopped moving.

"It is over." Greg and I embrace and weep.

Date of death: January 10, 2014
Time of death: 6:15 pm.
Ron is 83 years 4 months and 15 days old.

Ron fought a long hard fight. Although we were very sad, Greg and I both had feelings of relief. Not for ourselves only, we were glad for Ron. He finally did leave his earthly body and reached his eternal home! The weary and suffering expression that we had watched on Ron's thin sunken face disappeared! The skin became soft and his countenance was one of peace.

I left the room and notified the staff.

Twan and Connie arrive an hour and a half later. There is a quiet gasp from them both as they walk into the room.

"Poor Ron," they sigh. "He looks so thin, so different."

Connie brought Ron a card containing photos of him. They picture a happy Ron, enjoying past moments with friends and family. Ron's grandchildren loved him dearly. Although the pictures are too late for Ron to see, they mean a lot to me. They show many happy and good times of the past. Times which I had almost forgotten.

May Ron rest in peace.

One might ask, "Does it make sense, that a person could live life like the devil and with total disregard for others, yet still go to Heaven?" This question has been asked throughout the centuries.

I believe that it is the grace of God and the blood of Christ that cleanses us from our sin. The only requirement to get the golden ticket is to confess your faith in Jesus, to trust in Him and His work. The work was accomplished by way of the cross.

Those of us who are Christians experience the benefits and joyous life that can be. That is, those of us who live directed by the Spirit of God and have a personal relationship with God.

I am sure that you will agree, a person might confess, "Jesus Christ is Lord" and see no change. Unless the person dies to self and allows Christ to reign, they are living as almost separated from God. For the Spirit filled Christian, separation from God would be and is hell on earth!

Chapter 39
Paul Passes

As I put the finishing touches on *A Suzie Story,* I receive word that Paul is on his deathbed. I am in Texas writing and helping Mother. It has been ten months since Ron's death and I have had about all the death I want for a while.

The kids all rush to Paul's bedside. They have maintained contact with their real dad and visit him often. Now he is lying before them in a coma.

"When we turn off the machine he will pass on," the doctor tells Twan, Connie, and Jerome. There is no doubt they love him dearly. Paul Murphy entered this world alone and unwanted. He is not leaving that way.

The lights go out on the machines as each is unplugged or turned off. Only the heart monitor screen above the bed shows the peaks and valleys of a green line jumping up and down with each heartbeat. Reverently and expectantly, they watch and wait. And wait. And wait. They did not turn off one machine.

"I wonder if his pacemaker makes a difference."

Obituary:

Paul J Murphy, 79, died after a long illness in Tucson on Thursday Sept. 18, 2014.

He was a friend to many and never met a person he considered a stranger.

He was most proud of his family and traveled around the world with them.

Paul lived in Sierra Vista and is survived by his son, Jerome and wife Michelle and Paul's two grandchildren, Jacob and Evie. He is also survived by two other children, Twan Murphy and Connie Lober, both of Agoura Hills, Calif.; and five other grandchildren, Dalys Domm, Alyssa Domm, Sebastian Schroder, Benjamin Lober, Leola Lober; and one ex-wife.

Paul James Murphy
May 3, 1935 – September 18, 2014

Chapter 40
Epilogue

Life is simply a collage of many short stories! Everyone has a story to tell.

God has taught me the straight and narrow path through my mistakes, stubbornness and bad choices. The amazing thing is the straight and narrow path can be a fascinating highway, sometimes broad and unpredictable!

"Suzie, you make all of your experiences look inviting. It's as though you see God even in your muck and mire." I hear this often and it is true!

If the words on the previous pages indicate that I have had a chaotic roller coaster life, I agree! Not all experiences were remarkable, but there is a common thread throughout my life. That golden thread is my daily walk with my Lord and Savior.

As I forge ahead today, I am blessed and walk in splendid health. Each day begins a new story and the direction it takes is up to me! I continue to choose the roller-coaster lifestyle. Although my permanent residence is in California, near the Pacific Ocean, Texas will forever be my other retreat. Once a Texan, always a Texan.

Whether I am traveling or spending a few days near my Oxnard home, I continue to enjoy people and I try to touch others in encouraging and positive ways.

My Christian life is not a smooth journey that will calmly end at a funeral with me spiritually waving goodbye to family and friends. Instead, I will slide in with an earthshaking cloud of dust. When the dust settles, I will be standing in a tired and worn out body. "What a ride!" I will gladly say, as I slip into my new heavenly body and head off to the Promised Land.

I most certainly must add, "Thank you Lord for escorting me all the way." Thank you for reading my memoirs. My life and writing is far from over!

Suzie Cole

If you have enjoyed reading Suzie's story, find *A Suzie Story* on www.Amazon.com and leave many stars and a good review. Reviews and sales are what keep a writer writing!